DOCUMENT CONTROL

LIFECYCLE AND THE GOVERNANCE CHALLENGE

DAWIT KASSA

Dawit Kassa
Copyright © 2016. All rights reserved.

This book remains the copyrighted property of the author. No part of this book may be reproduced or redistributed to others for commercial or non-commercial purposes in any form or by any means, electronic or mechanical, without written permission from the author, except for the inclusion of brief quotations in a review

ISBN-13: 978-1519760456

Legal Disclaimer

This work is the individual property of the author and does not reflect the views or practices of his employers, clients or business partners.

Document control knowledge and best practices change constantly. Changes in organizations' document control requirements, advances in information technology, and new legal developments all profoundly affect the evolution of document control practices.

Practitioners and researchers must always rely on their own knowledge and experience in analyzing and applying any information or method described in this book.

To the fullest extent of the law, neither the Publisher nor the author, contributors or editors or anyone associated with the writing or publishing of this book assumes any liability for any injury and/or damage to persons or property as a matter of product liability, negligence or otherwise, or from any use of any methods, products, instructions or ideas contained in the material herein.

To my wife Emnet Yeshaneh

CONTENTS

Acknowledgments

Preface

1. Documents

Documents, Records and Uncontrolled Documents 3

Relationship between Documents and Records 8

Documents Types and Classifications 9

2. Document Control

Why Control Documents 14

The Document Control Environment 17

Document Control Principles 23

Origin of Document Control Requirements 25

3. Document Lifecycle

Creation 29

Review and Approval 32

Usage 41

Archival and Disposal 44

4. Document Control Governance

Document Control Strategy and Plan 50

Document Control Process and Procedure 52

Governing Document Control Instruments 55

Document Control Organization 58

The Role of the Document Controller 59

5. Document and Revision Numbering

Considerations in Document Numbering Design   65

Alternative Document Numbering Schemes   70

Document Revision Numbering   76

6. Document Templates

Why Use Templates   82

Template Parts   83

Creating and Using Document Templates   87

Success Factors In Using Templates   89

7. Document Quality Assurance and Control

Document Control Challenges   91

Quality Assurance and Control   93

Performance Indicators   98

8. Document Control Procedures

Writing an Effective Document Control Procedure   106

Qualities of a Good Procedure   109

Ensuring Sustained Compliance to Procedure   111

9. Project Document Control

The Project Environment   114

Document Lifecycle in Projects   118

Document Transmittals and Document Distribution   122

Project Document Control Activities   124

Challenges in Project Document Control   134

The Author

Index

ACKNOWLEDGMENTS

Writing this book was never a lonely journey. I had great support from a number of document control professionals. They came from different countries and industries, and spent many months and countless hours reviewing and commenting on the book. Their insights and encouragement truly made a difference.

I'm deeply grateful to all those who helped with making this book a reality. My special thanks goes to Ophélie Cassegrain, Adewuya Gbemisola Anthonette and Cindy Li Tang for their contributions and enthusiasm throughout the review and editing of the book.

PREFACE

The journey to this book started almost by accident. In early 2014, I noticed that there were not many books on general document control. In fact, the only book I could find was basic and was eight years old. So I decided to write small articles and share them with readers online.

Before I knew it, the articles morphed into a series of topics and chapters, and finally, after a year and half of writing, into this humble book.

This book presents many topics including the document lifecycle, document control process, governance and challenges, and provides practical advice on a number of topics. I am particularly hoping that new and mid-career document control professionals as well as anyone interested in document control will find it useful.

There is no doubt that document control is a vast discipline. Even though key document control activities appear similar across various industries, there can still be striking differences in certain areas. That makes capturing all document control topics in such a small book a challenge.

Nevertheless, the book presents specific topics such as project document control, and discusses various practices and approaches to a number of document control issues. Thanks to the many document control professionals that voluntarily reviewed and edited this book and are outside my immediate professional circle, I hope you will benefit from their experiences and perspectives on a number of topics.

My vision for this book is that it will gradually grow and evolve over time to address more document control topics, and become a handbook of document control. That will require additional insights into document control practices and that is where I need your help. If you have comments and suggestions to improve this book, please send them to me at thedocumentcontrolbook@gmail.com. I wish you a great read and I hope you will enjoy reading the book as much I did writing it.

CHAPTER 1

DOCUMENTS

Every time I think about the human past and present, I am fascinated by how much we have always been interested in documenting our journey in life.

I am amazed by prehistoric humans in Spain and Australia who left behind wall paintings 40,000 years ago. Egyptians, as early as the fourth millennium BCE, chronicled their lives and important historical events on papyrus and later on parchment. Assyrians of Mesopotamia and Babylonians used clay tablets to tell us about themselves well before the third millennium BCE. Many other civilizations used stone carvings to do the same. Without a doubt, documents–in one form or another–have been an important part of human history.

Given our current computerized world and widespread use of electronic documents, the business of documentation has become much more sophisticated.

The invention of the movable type printing press by Johannes Gutenberg in 1450 in Germany arguably kick started the printing revolution. At least in the longer run, it made document production easier, quicker and less costly. Gutenberg must have been very grateful to the Han Dynasty in China that invented paper at the beginning of the second century CE.

After all, because of the Chinese we have paper, and because of paper and printing we will always remember Gutenberg.

More recently, important historical and economic events such as the industrial revolution, emergence of multinational firms and globalization expanded the reach of companies across continents. Both small and large companies' started to produce countless products and sell them internationally where market boundaries became blurred. Competition became global, business regulation became tighter, and awareness of quality and safety grew. All these related factors led to an increased need for stricter quality management and its documentation.

Similarly, the evolution of the document management practice, the emergence of documentation professional institutions, and the development of information sciences in the past century shaped the writing and management of documents as a distinct discipline. But, perhaps most importantly, the advent of personal computers in the late 1970s and then the Internet had the biggest impact. Both of these important developments transformed document creation, storage, distribution and management.

The use of documents is now ubiquitous. Documents and records are at the heart of communication and governance in every organization. They are actively used not only to note what has happened but also to provide guidance on the execution of business activities and processes.

Documentation is key to retaining and transferring knowledge to others. It allows people to find answers easily instead of asking co-workers or constantly reinventing the wheel. It forms memories of the organization, and serves as evidence of business activities and compliance with rules and regulations.

In short, every organization–whether large or small, private or state-owned, project or manufacturing plant–depends on documents and records to sustain its operations.

However, before we dive into document control, let us first lay a good foundation for our discussion by answering the following key questions:

- What is a document?
- What are the differences between records and documents?
- Are they related in any way?

DOCUMENTS, RECORDS AND UNCONTROLLED DOCUMENTS

Strictly speaking, any enterprise's documentation is composed of documents, records, and uncontrolled documents, which are all different. This may seem unimportant and merely a matter of semantics. However, recognizing the differences and relationships is very important in order to fully understand the scope of document control and your role in it.

Documents

We know that the word 'document' comes from the Latin 'Documentum', which means lesson or instruction. Traditionally, the word 'document' referred to a paper-based textual record that is created or received as evidence of a business decision, interaction or aspiration. Over the years, many writers and researchers have offered their views on what a document is and what it is not. The meaning of documents has evolved over time. However, a consensus on what a document really is has been elusive.

For example, some writers asserted that any object that has fixity, materiality and intentionality as evidence can be regarded as a 'document' if one can be informed by observing it. This particular thinking, of course, led to a humorous argument that an antelope running wild in the plains of Africa can be considered a document if it were captured and put under scientific observation.

Joking aside, when computers started making their way into the work place, the definition of documents needed to be extended beyond traditional paper. Accordingly, electronic documents (by definition anything that can be file-named and kept on electronic media) were added to the list of documents. Similarly, with the increased use of audio-visual materials for work purposes, the meaning of documents was further broadened to include digital images, voice and video recordings.

Documents are now understood to be anything used to provide direction for performing work, making decisions, or exercising judgment which affects the safety or quality of goods and services.

Documents, unlike records, are forward looking and guide the organizations' business and technical decisions. Documents tell you what to do. Records say what was done. Common examples of documents are quality assurance policies and manuals, standard operating procedures (SOP), work instructions, engineering drawings, process descriptions, and product specifications.

The use of the wrong document for business will negatively affect product quality and could have negative consequences for production efficiency, and even for the health and safety of employees and consumers. For the same reason, you can't expect your customer to accept a product manufactured based on an outdated specification.

Therefore, all documents need to be kept up-to-date and strictly controlled throughout their lives. Any changes that are made must be reviewed and approved by authorized persons before the new content can be used. This is the reason why documents are also known as 'controlled documents.' Controlled documents have a unique identifier number, title, date of writing or approval, and the names of people responsible for their review and sign off. They also often have a signature, stamp, or special text on their cover pages to clearly differentiate them from records or uncontrolled documents.

But how do you know if a 'document' needs control in the first place? The rule of thumb is simple: a document needs to be controlled if the use of the wrong version would cause a quality, safety or compliance problem. That places the document control function at the center of quality assurance in many organizations.

Finally, it is important to note that documents are defined by their purpose and not just by their storage media. They can take various forms including written physical materials, electronic documents, photographs, microfilms, audio recordings, video tapes, CDs and DVDs, computer programs or even physical samples. In some industries, product models, soil and rock samples are considered documents because they inform the user what a good product or sample should look like. These documents will have to be treated just like any other if they are to be used for decision making.

Records

Records are often construed to mean evidence of a business activity or decision that happened in the past. They show if a process or an activity took place as intended. In essence, records are the organization's 'static' memories and need to be kept unchanged for future reference.

Examples of records are letters, invoices, receipts, reports, fulfilled contracts, test results, and completed daily maintenance logs.

You can see that records are historic in nature, and, therefore, unlikely to have a direct impact on the safety or quality of the organization's future activities. Since they normally don't require continued maintenance or updates like documents do, they are often stored and managed outside the document control environment. As a result, many organizations keep separate systems and processes to store and manage records.

However, the distinction between documents and records can be blurred at times.

For example, a standard quality control form is a controlled document. Why? Because you want to guide quality controllers on how to capture consistent quality data. But the moment the form is filled in, it becomes a record, and it will have to be moved to the records storage area. Similarly, documents such as plans, budget statements, contracts, and schedules lie somewhat on the borderline between documents and records. They are often created and managed as documents, but you know they will become historical like records when their intended timespan expires.

In the following chapters, you will see that when an existing document is reviewed and updated, the previous revision becomes outdated (i.e. a record). Such obsolete documents, even though they started their lives as proper documents, have to be removed from points of use, archived for record purposes and eventually destroyed. They are historical and no longer fit to guide business decisions.

To add to the vague distinction between documents and records, some organizations (especially projects) may decide to centrally register important records such as letters and reports, and even review and approve them in their document control systems together with controlled documents.

Such a practice clearly helps to centrally manage all documents and records in just one system. It results in the need for fewer personnel and lower system infrastructure costs. There is no question that both documents and records need to be stored and managed properly to ensure their retrievability, safety and security. However, the practice of managing records together with documents is not aligned with the idea of document control, which involves controlling and keeping documents up-to-date throughout their lives. This type of approach, in my opinion, can divert the focus of the document control function from quality assurance to records archival and retention. This can be a serious distraction, particularly if you run a manual document control process with significant documentation volume.

Nevertheless, in terms of conventional document control, 'to be' is to be a document. Records are dead, and uncontrolled documents (next section) don't even exist. Documents can be amended and improved, while records can't - unless authorized alterations are required to correct facts.

Uncontrolled documents

Uncontrolled documents include personal notes, work-in-progress documents, uncontrolled copies of documents or anything that is neither a controlled document nor a recognized record.

Uncontrolled documents are not meant or ready for making business and engineering decisions, nor are they evidence of a business transaction. Their quality is not assured and managed by document control. Consequently, their management is left to the individual or department that produces them.

Just like the difference between documents and records, the distinction between documents and uncontrolled documents is not always clear.

It is interesting to note that sometimes you may come across flip charts or white boards being used to provide certain instructions or even communicate schedule or production progress. Technically speaking, such materials, with the appropriate control, can be considered documents. But the reality is that ensuring the completeness, accuracy and timeliness of the information contained in such media can be very challenging for obvious reasons. That difficulty makes the use of such 'documents' unreliable.

Furthermore, as indicated earlier, controlled documents can become 'uncontrolled'. If a user, for instance, makes a copy of a controlled document and removes it from the document control library, the document can no longer be tracked, retrieved, updated, and quality-assured. Therefore, it becomes uncontrolled.

RELATIONSHIP BETWEEN DOCUMENTS AND RECORDS

The similarities and differences between documents and records are clear: records are static and historic, whereas documents are living materials that talk about actions in the future. Nevertheless, both require proper storage and management.

An important question to be asked is, is there any relationship between the two? The answer is yes. In fact, documents and records are complementary. They complement each other to tell a story about how well a process or an activity was carried out.

As shown in Figure 1.1, every process requires an input (e.g. labor, raw materials) which will be converted into an output (i.e. goods and services). For example, a spare parts manufacturer consumes steel and other materials, and converts them into finished parts through its production and assembly processes.

Documents enable smooth process execution because they contain vital information that guides the selection of inputs (e.g. an approved list of preferred suppliers), the conversion process (e.g. fabrication instructions) and even the management of the output (e.g. inventory management procedure). We all know that many processes in organizations are supported and guided by documents such as strategies, policies and procedures.

Records, on the other hand, tell you how well the guidelines and instructions in documents were applied, and how successful these documents were in managing the input, process, and output. Raw material inventory records, facilities maintenance logs, and finished product quality inspection reports are excellent examples of records on input, process, and output, respectively. Note that the results captured in records serve as feedback to improve the performance of the process.

From a documentation perspective, the input-process-output phases can be successfully executed only when document users fully understand this relationship. Users need to know which documents to use for which activity, and what records to produce as a result of performing that activity. Such requirements are communicated to users via documents.

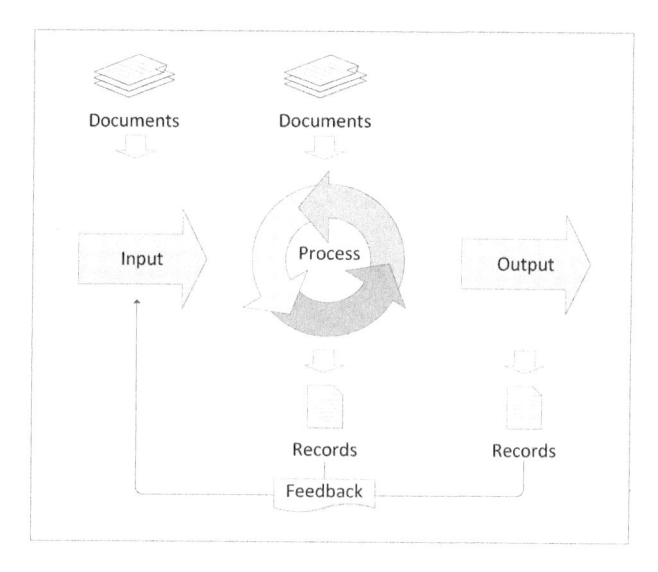

Figure 1.1: Simplified relationship between documents and records with the Input- Process-Output (IPO model)

To summarize, despite their differences, records and documents together provide the complete picture of how an organization performs it activities and what the outcomes are.

DOCUMENTS TYPES AND CLASSIFICATIONS

A common topic in document control is the types and classification of documents. Every organization needs a way to classify its documents so that they can be organized in a certain manner that makes document placement and retrieval more effective.

How documents should be organized depends on the company's unique requirements and circumstances. That means, as it is with many other document control topics, there is no one best way of doing it.

For instance, documents can be grouped as project and non-project documents. Project documents are created with a specific project in mind and are used during the project's life time. Non-project documents are those created and maintained to support the day-to-day operations of a non-project-based organization.

Documents can be of internal or external origin depending on who produces them. Internal documents are authored by the company while external documents are written and transferred to the company by external parties such as customers, suppliers, and contractors.

Documents can be of different types. The types of documents can include: management and administration, engineering and design, fabrication and assembly, operations and maintenance, quality assurance, contracting and procurement, finance and accounting, marketing, government and legal, and others depending on the purpose or origin of the documents.

Engineering documents include the engineering specifications, drawings, and technical illustrations that are prepared to establish the design of a product. Management and administrative documents comprise scheduling, planning, and organizational documents such as policies, rules, regulations, job descriptions, and training materials. Examples of quality assurance documents are the quality assurance policy, standards and procedures, work instructions, checklists, and forms defined to support the quality assurance and control function.

Fabrication and assembly documents are prepared to support the development and validation of whatever the organization or its contractors produce. Operations and maintenance documents are used to support the ongoing functioning and upkeep of the production facilities. Contracting and procurement documents guide the contractual interface with the contractors developing, manufacturing, and delivering goods and services to the organization. Other documents support financial, book keeping, regulatory, and legal decisions and activities. If the organization has a centralized document control system, then all these documents will be stored and controlled in this one environment.

Projects often classify their documents based on professional disciplines such as civil engineering, mechanical engineering, electrical engineering, finance, and so on. The 'Coding System' (Norsok Z-DP-002) standard from Norway provides a complete classification for project documents.

Information security-aware companies usually add another layer of document classification: confidential, private or public documents. This allows companies to organize and manage each document based on its level of confidentiality.

There may be other ways to classify and organize your documents. In any case, a good document classification should provide clear separation between different document classes and should allow users to efficiently store and retrieve documents.

Document Control

Chapter 2

Document Control

What is document control? How does it contribute to meeting business goals?

Good document control means that the right people create, review and approve relevant documents. As a result, users are provided with the latest revision of the documents they need. Unauthorized persons are prevented from accessing documents.

The ultimate purpose of document control is to assure the quality of goods and services that an organization produces. Document control helps prevent quality problems by providing a comprehensive framework and guidance for the creation and usage of documents. It allows you to manage documents through their lifecycle to a much higher degree of quality, availability, reliability and security. These documents are used to guide and assure the quality of company decisions and activities, which will ultimately impact product quality.

This chapter is intended to introduce you to fundamental document control topics that you will find useful to better understand the rest of the book. We will start with why we need to control documents, and then discuss the cornerstones of an effective document control environment. We will also see the principles behind document control, and where some of the most common document control requirements come from. These topics will apply to your document control practice regardless of which industry or project you are engaged in.

WHY CONTROL DOCUMENTS

In this era of knowledge, every organization is driven by information. Up-to-date information is required to make good business decisions: from the making of competitive products to distribution to the right market.

For any company to succeed in the long run, it must give emphasis to quality and compliance. Ensuring quality and compliance requires providing employees and partners with the right guidance so they can adhere to quality and compliance requirements. Providing clear document guidance usually involves the use of documents.

Good document control helps prevent product quality, safety and health problems by minimizing the risk of document inaccuracy, document loss and information security violations. Without documents and effective document control, companies would struggle to achieve their quality and compliance objectives. Therefore, having the right documentation available at the right time and place may very well determine any organization's survival.

Other ways that document control can help your organization are discussed below.

Reduced cost of compliance

Regulators determine many aspects of companies' compliance to quality through the inspection of documents whose review and approval audit trail is managed by document control. Unfortunately, inefficient document control is among the greatest detriments to compliance for companies doing business in regulatory environments.

The US Food and Drug Administration (FDA) reports that poor documentation of training activities, bad raw material handling policies and practices, and poor use of sign-off logs are some of the most commonly food safety issues that are faced by the food processing industry today. The FDA, an agency of the US Department of Health and

Human Services, works to protect public health by regulating the safety and quality of food items, human and veterinary drugs, biological products, medical devices, tobacco and cosmetics products and products that emit radiation.

Better communication and knowledge management

Effective document control not only reduces your costs of compliance with state and international regulations, but also helps you proactively improve process and product quality through the appropriate documentation and communication of good practices. Document control provides written, quality assured and approved documents that replace verbal instructions which are often not heard, misunderstood, quickly forgotten or ignored.

Clear and well written documents such as policies, procedures, and technical specifications are great examples of tools that help organizations communicate effectively among their staff and customers. Such documents help staff to cooperate better by understanding and undertaking critical processes consistently without the need for repeated verbal communication.

Good document control also supports effective and efficient organizational activities by providing employees, customers, and business partners with access to quality and up-to-date documents. It helps to avoid confusion among writers and users about document revisions and their locations by making only the latest revision of each document centrally available at a point in time.

In addition, in the field of research and development, documents help materialize concepts, ideas, studies, and results into knowledge that can be communicated to others. Documents make the preservation of know-how and achievements possible, and document control allows users to easily access the documented knowledge in the future.

Standardization of document review and approval

Document control practices may differ from company to company depending on the company's line of business, the complexity of its operations and the associated risks among other factors.

A well-designed and communicated document control process improves users' confidence in the quality of documents. That is achieved by standardizing the review, approval, and distribution of documents throughout the organization.

One good example is the 'red lining' of design drawings. This is a decades-old standard process of capturing changes to drawings which result from actual construction alterations. Engineers often use red, blue, and green colors to indicate deletions, additions, and other comments. To this date, however, there is no industry agreement on which color represents what. In fact, some companies use a red color to denote all changes. In such cases, a well-defined document control process and procedure helps to clarify such issues and establish standard practices.

Reduction of document search and retrieval time

Imagine an enormous room full of cardboard document boxes or rows of filing cabinets. Your task is to find a document you urgently need. You have no idea where to start or if you are in the right storage room to begin with. You are not even sure if the document is in the library. Unfortunately, this is a reality for many companies.

Centrally storing the latest revision of documents in an organized manner and being able to retrieve them quickly helps users save the time they would otherwise spend looking or asking around for documents. It helps them to minimize misfiling or loss of documents, and saves time and effort that would be required to find or recreate them. That improves staff productivity and helps you avoid fines, plant shutdowns, and litigation expenses as a result of using the wrong documents.

Safety and security of documents

Information security is high on the agenda of many firms, particularly among those that deal with proprietary technology or confidential information. In this regard, good document control is essential in order to keep documents safe from unauthorized access, and to ensure that only the right people have the proper level of access to confidential documents.

Document control also ensures that documents are protected from damage and destruction by fire, flood or other means. Document controllers are expected to make recommendations to management so that the necessary document safeguarding processes, equipment and technology (e.g. fire proof file cabinets, smoke detectors in libraries, etc.) are put into place.

THE DOCUMENT CONTROL ENVIRONMENT

Any document control environment consists of three distinct, and yet closely related and complex elements: people, process, and technology. These elements form the cornerstones of any document control environment, and all three need to be carefully defined and managed to enable an effective and customer-oriented document control function.

People

The 'people' element is about individuals' roles and responsibilities in managing documents. Document control can be a complex process that involves a number of participants both inside and outside of your organization.

Common document control roles include document originator, reviewer, approver, user and document controller, who are all in one way or another involved in the creation, quality assurance, sign-off and management of documents.

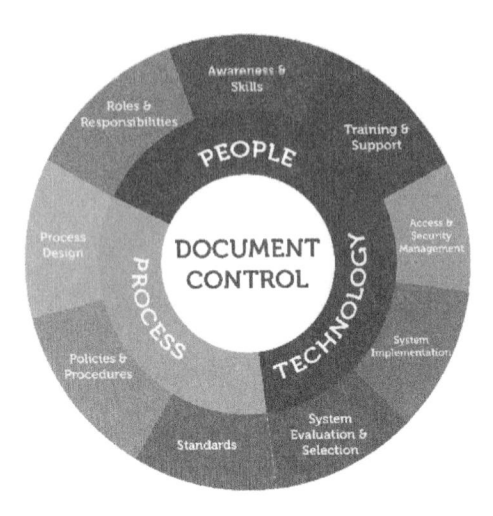

Figure 2.1: The People-Process-Technology interaction in document control

A document originator is a person tasked with drafting a new document or re-writing an existing one. The originator, also known as document writer, responsible engineer or simply author, is responsible for the content and delivery of the document. He ensures that the document's purpose and content are clearly defined; the document is subject to an appropriate level of review; reviewers' comments are incorporated into the document; evidence of the review process is documented, and that the necessary approvals are obtained before the document can be released for use.

The document reviewer reads and analyses a draft document prepared by the document originator. At the end of the document review process, the reviewer provides the originator with comments and suggestions required to improve and make the document meet the minimum acceptable quality standards. Document reviewers are often qualified personnel such as process owners or skilled users that are most affected by the document and that have the required training and experience to review documents written in their area of expertise. A single document can be reviewed by two or more reviewers.

Once a document has been reviewed, and the reviewers' comments are incorporated, it goes to the document approver. The approver reads the document carefully and signs off on it if he agrees with the quality of the document and has no comments. If the approver sees significant quality issues with the document, the document will then need to be further improved by the originator according to the approver's comments. The approver is accountable for the quality of the document and authorizes the document by wet-signing it physically or digitally. In some cases, a document may require the signature of two or more approvers before it can be released for use.

A related role to the approver is the document owner role. The document owner is the manager or representative of the department that is responsible for making sure the document is always up-to-date. Document owners are often approvers since they are the subject matter experts or process owners of the matter the document addresses, and therefore, are qualified to approve or reject the document after review. Document owners/approvers are also responsible for identifying qualified document reviewers and are actively involved in the review and approval of documents.

Document users are seldom included in the discussion on document control roles and responsibilities. Often, they are regarded as dormant document readers with no obligations or contributions towards effective document control. However, the fact is that document control and use is everyone's responsibility and users have an important part to play.

Users are expected to not only use the latest document for their work and dispose of older revisions, but also to inform the originator if the contents of a document are unclear or incorrect. Internal users, in particular, are expected to work closely with document originators by sharing with them their valuable knowledge on the subject. Experienced document originators know that the best documents are written in collaboration with users and process owners – whether it is the mechanic at the shop floor, or the operator in the control room.

As an example, users need to be aware that if they distribute a document, they are responsible for controlling its distribution. The original author or document controller won't know who has distributed copies of their documents, so they can't control such document distribution. Accordingly, users need to be appropriately informed and trained to effectively carry out their document control responsibilities.

Last but not least, document controllers are responsible for ensuring the health of the document control process so that it works as intended. They verify, register, file and distribute documents in compliance with the document control procedure. They manage the access, storage and archival of documents.

Larger organizations have a lead document control position known as document coordinator. The coordinator is responsible for managing both internal and external document control relationships. He implements the document control processes and systems and ensures the completeness and accuracy of document registers. He also actively participates in document control-related meetings and anticipates and plans for the document management needs of the organization.

The document coordinator also measures progress in the completion of deliverables, and issues document control reports. In projects, the document coordinator is responsible for comprehending and enforcing the document management requirements as per the contract together with the client or contractor. The coordinator designs document control training and trains users and document controllers. In smaller organizations where there is only a document controller, the controller will have to double-hat the coordinator's role.

Table 2.1 summarizes the responsibilities of the various roles we just discussed. It is important to remember that the roles discussed above can be internal or external to your organization. Among external document control participants are your customers, suppliers (e.g. designers, manufacturers and suppliers), joint-venture partners and international or local regulators.

External customers either provide you with documents such as product specifications, or they are involved in the process by reading the user manuals or drawings produced by your company. Suppliers provide you with goods and services required for your processes according to your specifications. International standards setting organizations such as ISO set the document control requirements which you may have to comply with. Local regulatory bodies may also require you to involve them in the creation and approval of certain documents.

Process

The document control process refers to the series of steps and actions involved in managing documents through their lifecycle. The process includes document creation, review, approval, and archival, and is discussed in detail in the next chapter.

To a large extent, the success of document control relies on the process behind it. It is essential that you have a well-defined, documented, and communicated document control process that is supported by appropriate procedures, instructions, templates and training materials.

Your document control process needs to be consistent with your business strategy, processes, requirements and unique circumstances. The document control process needs to be flexible so that it allows the smooth flow of various documents to completion. A stringent process that requires all documents to go through the same series of activities (e.g. if approval and signatures for a simple form is expected from a senior manager as normally is for a policy) can end up causing a bottleneck and frustration among document writers and users.

Activity	Originator	Reviewer	Approver/ Owner	User	Document controller
Initiate document change	Responsible	Consulted	Accountable	Consulted	None
Write document	Responsible	Informed	Accountable	Consulted	None
Select reviewers and approvers	Responsible/ Consulted	Informed	Accountable/ Responsible	Informed	Informed
Review document	Consulted	Responsible	Informed	Responsible if they are reviewers	Informed
Incorporate comments	Responsible	Consulted	Consulted	None	None
Approve document	Informed	Informed	Responsible	Informed	Informed
Distribute document	Consulted	Informed	Informed	Informed	Responsible
Archive/destroy document	Informed	Informed	Accountable	Responsible for disposing of old revisions	Responsible

Table 2.1: RACI (Responsible-Accountable-Consulted-Informed) chart of document lifecycle management roles

Remember, even though key document control principles remain similar among different industries, each organization still needs to design its own fit-for-purpose processes that are suited to the unique opportunities and challenges it faces.

Technology

Important topics in technology within the context of document control are the identification, evaluation, selection and implementation of document creation and management systems, and their day-to-day management including audits and security management.

A number of technologies can be employed in a single document control environment. The technology to write and edit documents can range from modest paper and pen to the latest drawing and publishing software. Document indexing and storage facilities can be as sophisticated as the latest Internet-based electronic document management systems (EDMS) or as simple as a filing cabinet.

Increasingly, however, more large organizations are switching to electronic solutions including EDMS in order to centralize their documents and to automate document storage and retrieval. At the same time, the document control technology continues to evolve with smarter solutions and newer players joining the market regularly.

This book will focus more on the 'people' and 'process' aspects which in my view are more fundamental than technology for document control.

DOCUMENT CONTROL PRINCIPLES

There are certain principles that form the basis for any document control process and ensure its usability and integrity. These principles are discussed throughout this book, and will be summarized here.

Identification of documents

This is the very basic principle of controlling a document. If you can't uniquely identify a document, you can't control it!

Every controlled document needs to have certain identifiers which are normally given to the document during its initial writing. The very unique identifying detail for any document is its document number. A document number is a distinctive number or alpha-numeric combination that is given exclusively to a single document and no other in a certain document repository.

Other important document identifying details, though not necessarily unique, are the document title, document type, revision number and date of revision.

These details will allow users to differentiate between documents and even between different revisions of a document. These and other pieces of information such as the names of the originator and approver are usually kept on the cover page of the document for easy identification. The document number, revision number and date can be included at the header or footer of every page. This will help with the easy identification of a document if the cover page is lost or a single page goes loose.

Central management of documents

It is important to control and manage all master documents centrally. This is the central idea of document control. Centralizing document storage allows you to monitor the quality of documents, to manage access and to always ensure you never lose original documents. The identification and removal of obsolete documents also become easier if your documents are centrally managed.

A centralized document management means that every original copy of a document always stays at the document center (file cabinet or EDMS) and is not issued to users or made available for unauthorized change.

Nevertheless, controlled copies of original documents can be made available to users at points of use (e.g. at the shop floor) in order to enable easy access to documents. These copies will be registered by the document controller and replaced with newer copies every time a new revision of the original document is released.

Documented process and procedure

As said earlier, effective document control requires a documented process and supporting procedures. The process and procedure should be tailored to the needs of the organization that uses them. Document control processes need to be practical and the procedures need to be documented and communicated to the various document control participants. No document process is useful if it is not explicitly documented and made part of the daily routine.

Tracking of change

Documents can be modified and updated over their lifecycle. Since the quality of documents has a direct impact on the quality of products, the changes made to documents need to be monitored and documented.

For audit and compliance purposes, it is important to keep the required details on what has changed in the new document revision. The retained details should at least state the time and nature of the change (e.g. update, addition or deletion) along the names of the originator and approver. All these details are normally captured by what is known as a revision record sheet which is part of many document templates.

ORIGIN OF DOCUMENT CONTROL REQUIREMENTS

Whether you are a small or multinational company, a struggling entrepreneur or an industry leader, you may need to adhere to certain industry and regulatory document control standards in order to succeed at what you do.

Document control standards and practices are driven primarily by the requirement to ensure quality and safety of company business processes and products. A good understanding of the applicable standards and requirements will enable you to establish best practices and help you to sustain and grow your business under a certain set of guidelines. For that to happen, all mandatory requirements need to be carefully identified and embedded into the document control process and procedure. But what are these standards?

Document control requirements come from three main sources:

- The state or government
- International or industry standards
- Your own organization or project requirements

State or government requirements are part of the law and are, therefore, compulsory. A good example is the documentation requirements of the United States Food and Drug Administration (FDA). The FDA regulations require companies to manage documents such as standard operating procedures (SOPs) and design history files (DHFs) so that businesses' quality management systems can be made safe, reliable and auditable when required.

Similarly, many other countries have a number of laws which dictate how documents should be controlled. The Canadian Quality Assurance and Control Standards are an example. There may be federal and state legislation in the country of your operation or market which must be fully understood and complied with. Violation of such document control standards can lead to the stripping of the company's license to operate, or may even result in a complete shutdown.

The International Organization for Standardization, popularly known as ISO, is perhaps the most recognized and accepted body for setting international quality standards including those for document control. Compliance with these standards is not mandatory unless your company wants to obtain an ISO certification. Many companies prefer to be ISO-certified, since these quality certifications give companies an edge over competitors by creating customer trust.

Among the ISO standards, ISO 9000 deals with the essentials of quality management systems including the eight management principles upon which the family of standards is based. ISO 9001 details the requirements that organizations wishing to meet the standard must fulfill. Specifically, ISO 9001:2008 (Quality Management Systems – Requirements), Clause 4.2 requires the establishment of a document control process whose purpose is to store and manage documents (such as the quality assurance policy) which are related to the implementation, maintenance, and continuous improvement of a quality management system. Clause 4.2 further demands that documents be reviewed and approved before use. It also requires that documents be legible, up-to-date, communicated, readily available at points of use, and removed from use when they become obsolete. The clause also mandates that documents of external origin be identified and their distribution managed.

Similarly, many other parts of the ISO 9001:2008 require organizations to do things that are also part of the document control function. For example, Clauses 8.5.2 and 8.5.3 mandate the need to document and maintain procedures to prevent and correct quality nonconformities.

In Europe, Standards Norway is responsible for all standardization areas except electro-technology and telecommunication in Norway. It adopts and publishes many new standards yearly based on national, European and International standards. For example, the 'Coding System' standard (Norsok Z-DP-002) prescribes document classification, project document numbering codes, and codes for document revision, status and acceptance.

More stringent document control requirements may come from a number of other sources including customers and internal business processes. For example, design and construction contractors are often asked to control their documents in the client's preferred way. These requirements may involve the use of a defined document control process, a specific document numbering scheme, document monitoring and reporting mechanisms, EDMS, certain templates, etc.

If you are in a new department or business within a large, long-standing company, you might also want to align and standardize with the document control practices of your peers. This might mean anything from sharing of existing document templates to complying with standing document control processes and systems.

Likewise, the volume of documents and the complexity of a company's operations may dictate the document control process and the technology selection. Companies or projects that operate in multiple locations are good examples. They often use Internet-based EDMSs and the associated processes since EDMSs provides access to the same document over the Internet in all corners of the world.

Chapter 3

Document Lifecycle

All documents are born, live for some time, retire and eventually die.

Documents can have an active and dynamic life. Once created, they will be reviewed, approved and updated several times. When they become obsolete, they will be archived and eventually disposed of when no longer needed. This set of life stages that documents pass through is known as the document lifecycle. It is essential that each stage of a document's lifecycle be managed well for the document to meet minimum quality requirements and serve its purpose.

This chapter details the different stages of the document lifecycle.

CREATION

From document control perspective, a document comes into existence when it is introduced into the register of the document control center. This occurs when the document is given its identifying details such as document title and number, and is registered on the master document register (MDR), which lists all controlled documents within a company or a project.

There are two ways that a document can come into being. One is when a new document is registered and distributed for review. For example, an engineer drafts a new drawing which will then be registered by the document controller and issued for comment by design review engineers. Some organizations require that a document creation form be completed and approved by the right authority before document writing can begin. This ensures that the creation of new documents is supported by good reasoning and that unnecessary, duplicated or overlapping documents are minimized.

The second route to document 'creation' is when a document is received from a source external to the organization. An example is when a customer's product specification is received, registered and stored in the central document repository to be used for product manufacturing.

To enable effective document identification and use, each document needs to have a unique title and identifying number, revision code, date of preparation or approval, purpose of issue (i.e. for review, approval, or for information, etc.), document type identifier, and names of people who wrote (originator), reviewed (reviewers) and approved (approver) the document. All of these details are kept on the cover page of the document, often in the revision record table. Details such as document title, number, revision code and date can also be made available in the header or footer of each page of the document.

An important aspect of the document writing is the use of templates. Document templates standardize document layout and help maintain minimum document quality standards. A good document control environment will have ready-made standard templates and will require all document originators to use them consistently. The use of templates is further discussed in Chapter Six.

Unfortunately, many document quality issues start with the wrong use of templates or poor document writing. Many times originators use outdated templates, don't provide all the required document identifying details or simply write unnecessarily lengthy or poorly drafted documents. Document reviewers, approvers, users and controllers have the responsibility to challenge and help improve document content that does not meet the organization's minimum document standards. For example, document controllers can make use of a checklist of criteria which a document needs to meet before it can be accepted by the document control center.

Rev. No.	Issue Date	Purpose	Author	Reviewer	Approver
1R	14.07.2014	Issued for Review	Ron Rene	Dick Smith	

Figure 3.1: Sample revision record table

Another important consideration in document creation is the naming of your documents. Documents need to be given descriptive titles that clearly indicate their content. Use of vague titles and terms such as 'miscellaneous' should be avoided. Whenever possible, each title should be unique and consistent so that users can easily search and find documents without confusion by identical document titles. For instance, if you name a procedure 'Procedure for Employee Selection' then consistently name your other procedures 'Procedure for' this and that. If you are new to the organization, check the document control procedure or ask your team for a document naming standard, a list of terms or naming acronyms that are already established and in use.

If you are using EDMS, which by default requires you to assign filenames to your documents during registration in the system, use the actual title of the document as the filename without special characters like &, - , :, ?, @, and #. Special characters are rejected by some computer systems, and you will have problems especially if your documents are to be shared with external partners such as clients. Moreover, ensure that the document's filename is the same as the document's title to enhance document search and retrieval. If a date or revision code is an important component of the filename, use a standard format such as 'YYYYMMDD' or '01R' and keep it consistent.

Once documents are created they will be reviewed, re-reviewed and approved as many times as required throughout their lifecycle.

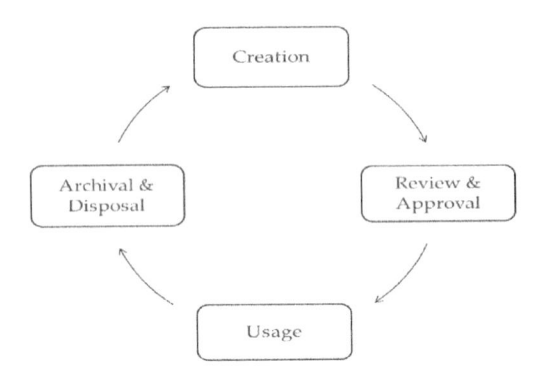

Figure 3.2: The document lifecycle

REVIEW AND APPROVAL

Document review

Documents require review and updating for a number of reasons.

A newly drafted drawing, for instance, needs to be reviewed by qualified engineer(s) for quality assurance purposes before it can be approved and released for use.

Similarly, a document that contains outdated, incorrect or ambiguous information needs to be updated with the latest information. Business standards, practices, regulations, specifications and circumstances outside the company change from time to time, and your documents need to reflect the latest changes.

The document review process ensures that the document is carefully analyzed and commented upon by authorized and qualified document reviewers. It further ensures that the document, based on the comments received, is amended by the originator to meet the minimum quality standards in terms of information accuracy and completeness. A good document review process also helps document comment resolution for future reference and audit.

Some organizations mandate the use of a document change request form to keep track of why a document was changed. This practice requires change requestors to obtain approval from the responsible person or department before they initiate the review of an existing document. This ensures that only needed changes are made and that an audit trail is kept on the request and authorization of the change. A single form can be used to request the creation, change, cancellation, superseding or archival of documents. See Figure 3.3 for an example of a change request form.

A good document review practice recommends having at least two reviewers to assure the quality of a document. In large businesses, reviewers of a particular document usually include at least the process owner (i.e. person responsible for that business process or part of the organization), the company subject matter expert (SME) on the topic the document covers, the prospective users of the document and when required the Quality Assurance and Control (QA&C) officer. The key is keeping the balance between the right groups of reviewers and having too many reviewers commenting on a single document.

In a project environment, a large number of people from different teams may be required to review a document. In such cases, the originator and approver of the documents should carefully select from each team, representatives called focal points. The nominated focal point will be responsible for distributing the document within their team, and filtering and consolidating feedback before passing it to the originator. This arrangement ensures that the comments are discussed and agreed upon by the team before they reach the originator. It also helps prevent the document from being lost deeper into the review team's organization. The focal point, in this sense, takes the 'document controller' role ensuring that the team finalizes their review on time.

Document Control

DOCUMENT CHANGE REQUEST FORM	
Date: DD/MM/YYYY	Change Request No:
Originator Name:	Originator Signature:
Affected Document: Title: Doc No: Revision No:	Other Documents Affected: Doc No: Doc No: Doc No: Doc No:
Proposed Change: Continuation sheet(s) attached: ☐ Yes ☐ No	
Justification: Continuation sheet(s) attached: ☐ Yes ☐ No Page ___ of ___	
RESERVED FOR USE BY APPROVING AUTHORITY	
Date: DD/MM/YYYY	Decision: ☐ Accepted ☐ Rejected
Remark: Continuation sheet(s) attached: ☐ Yes ☐ No	
Approved by:	Signature:

Figure 3.3: Sample document change request form

That allows the originator to work with only the focal points instead of engaging each member of the multiple teams. In smaller organizational settings, the originator can be responsible for overviewing the review process.

The typical (non-project) document review process goes as follows.

A manager, as an example, drafts a new policy document which has to be reviewed by the appropriate people in the organization before it can be signed off on. The manager sends the document to the document controller for the purpose of registration and distribution to the appropriate reviewers. Once the reviewers receive the document, they go through it, and write down and pass their comments to the originator through the document controller before the due date.

The review process is increasingly done electronically in document management systems (EDMS). These systems enable you to electronically share documents for review and collect reviewers' comments in the same way.

In a paper-based document review scenario, the originator, with the help of the document controller, sends copies of the document and a document review form to the reviewers. The use of a standard document review form (also known as comments sheet, see Figure 3.4) guides the reviewers to provide comments in a consistent manner that they be easily consolidated without any ambiguity.

The originator then incorporates the relevant comments into the document and decides whether to send the next revision for another round of review or final approval. That decision depends on the complexity of the comments received, the maturity level of the document and the document control process (i.e. if all documents need to be issued for review once changes are made and before they can approved).

While accepting or rejecting reviewers' comments, it is a good practice to discuss the comments with each reviewer to further clarify their reasons, concerns or questions, and to let them know the reason why their comments are rejected. This proactive discussion could also provide the originator a conditional agreement from the reviewers on the way the comments should be included so that the document can be issued directly for approval next time, avoiding another round of document review on the newly made changes.

It is important to note that not all documents require reviewing or updating. A good example of such a document is a local government's standard procedure which your business must follow on a specific process. Such documents need to be 'approved' by the relevant person in your organization before they can be used. However, they don't require any review since they are meant to be used without any change to their content. Only the local government, in this case, can review and update the document.

Therefore, some organizations and regulations stipulate that certain documents must be reviewed within in certain amount of time.

Periodic review of documents is a proactive approach that helps to prevent quality problems by instilling a conscious culture of keeping documents up-to-date. The document control procedure or other company procedure needs to clearly identify which documents need to be reviewed, how often and exactly when. To that end, the document control procedure may include a document review schedule.

Documents may be reviewed periodically or randomly as necessary. In many dynamic business situations, there is a real danger of running into quality and safety issues as a result of using outdated documents that don't reflect changing business parameters.

An integral part of the review process is tracking the changes made to documents over their life time. Keeping a short record of what has changed in each new revision of a document enables readers to determine the changes in few seconds without the need to closely compare two revisions of the document.

\multicolumn{2}{c}{**DOCUMENT REVIEW FORM**}
Title:	Review Form No:
Doc No:	Date: DD/MM/YYYY
Revision No:	Reviewer Name:
Originator Name:	Reviewer Signature:

Review Outcome (Check only one):

☐ No Comments
☐ Comments - Response NOT Required (See comments below)
☐ Comments - Response Required (See comments below)

COMPLETE ONLY IF 'COMMENTS -RESPONSE REQUIRED' SELECTED

Response Agreed: ☐ Yes	Date: DD/MM/YYYY
Reviewer Signature:	Originator Signature:

REVIEWER COMMENTS

No	Page	Comment	Y/N	A/R	Comment Resolution	A/R

Continuation sheet(s) attached:
☐ Yes ☐ No Page __ of __

*Resp Req= Response Required   Y/N= Yes/No   A/R= Accepted/Rejected

Figure 3.4: Sample document review form

When making changes to large documents, it is important that the originator summarize the changes so readers know what has actually changed. Summarizing and recording document changes help reviewers and approvers to easily understand the changes made and to expedite the review and approval process. Providing visibility of the changes to a document also enables the document change initiators to easily confirm whether their proposed changes were used as intended. Furthermore, auditors benefit from a document change history because it enables them to easily identify and focus on the changes.

Document change tracking is done by keeping a change record as part of the document. The change record, also known as change table, can be a simple chart with columns for revision number or date of the document and a description of the change and the pages revised. Figure 3.5 shows a combined revision record and change table. The change table can also be kept separately, since it is often hard to keep all of the details including names and signatures of reviewers and approvers in just one row of a table. If it is not possible to keep the change record as part of the document itself, the changes can be stored elsewhere accessible to users. If you are using EDMS, the software may be able to store the change details in the database, and a change table may not be required on the document.

Another way to show the latest document changes to readers is to highlight the updated or new information in the document. This can be done by side-lining, underlining or boldfacing the change or by using a similar technique. Companies may also elect to append the change details to the initiating change request if there is one.

Lastly, whenever the next revision of a document is prepared, it will be issued with a new date, revision code and document status (e.g. issued for review and then approved for use). The purpose of these changes is to enable readers to differentiate between the most recent and older revisions of the same document. The most appropriate approach for formal documents, and for documents that require approval or review on a regular basis is to use revision numbers with decimals (e.g. 1.1, 1.2) in order to indicate minor changes and whole numbers (e.g. 1.0, 2.0) to indicate a release or approved revision.

Rev. No.	Issue Date	Purpose	Description of Revision Changes
1R	14.07.2014	Issued for Review	First issue
2A	31.07.2014	Approved for Use	Page 5- updated section 2.2 - list of emergency response equipment.
3R	15.06.2015	Issued for Review	Page 11- updated section 3.1 – location of emergency response equipment. Page 23- changed name and contact details of main emergency focal point

Figure 3.5: Sample revision record that includes change details

Document approval

A document will be issued for approval once it has gone through the required number of review cycles and after all relevant comments have been incorporated into the document.

The approval of the document assures the reader that the document has been formally reviewed and quality checked by the relevant quality authority in the organization. That means that the responsible authority agrees the document is ready for carrying out the work it is intended for without any further update.

Organizations usually require that a document be approved by a supervisor even when it seems like a process owner or a subject matter expert (SMEs) is the most qualified person to approve the document. This is because supervisors are ultimately accountable for the document's quality. In addition, compared to process owners and SMEs, supervisors have better visibility on the impact that related documents in the wider organization may have on the document under discussion.

An important decision that has to be made in writing documents is deciding who needs to approve and sign a controlled document. The absence of an important stakeholder from the signature list can later lead to quality problems since the signatories input has not been included or they may not agree with the content or quality of the document. On the other hand, requesting a signature that does not add value to the document is inefficient and causes delay. The rule of thumb is that every signature associated with a document's review and approval should add value to the document. It is the expectation that every individual who signs a document is well trained and authorized to do so.

Many firms require approved documents to be physically signed by the approver. In many cases, approvers can sign on the cover page of the document against their names, and the document can then be scanned and stored in EDMS, if you are using one. Signatures don't necessarily have to be handwritten since modern EDMSs allow for the digital signing of the documents. Emails can also be used as record of approval. They can be embedded in the document or archived separately to support the approval history. However, in some countries, certain documents (e.g. contractual documents) have to be wet-signed with permanent ink to meet regulatory requirements and need to be stored as hardcopies. The wet-signed original documents can be stamped, for example 'ORIGINAL' in red, to help identify the original version from other color copies.

When a document issued for review or approval reaches the required quality level, the approver notifies the originator that the document is ready for approval. The originator then updates the status of the document from 'Issued for Review' or 'Issued for Approval' to 'Approved' or 'Released,' and ensures that it is signed by the approver. Through the document controller, the originator then makes sure that the new document is distributed to users and old revisions are collected and archived. He or the document controller must also archive the document change request and comment forms for compliance reasons.

Of course, after some time most approved documents will once again need to enter the review and approval cycle for reasons mentioned in the previous section. This, in fact, can happen many times over the life of a document.

It has to be noted that reviewing and approving documents is just the first step in quality assurance. Whenever important changes are made to documents, users should be informed of the change and the organization should be made ready for the impact. For example, when required, the necessary instructions and training should be given to users of the document so that they will be able to apply the changes to their work and achieve the intended results. In fact, some EDMS systems trigger new training requirements to users of the document every time a change is made to it. Put simply, a change to a document is not complete until everyone whose work is affected by it understands the change and is prepared to implement it in his area of responsibility.

Sometimes the introduction of a new document comes with the introduction of a new process. To minimize the impact and to ensure a smooth transition, a document implementation plan may be required. Sometimes, a change to a document may trigger a change to other documents because the underlying business processes are linked to each other. Document originators and approvers, therefore, need to assess the effect of the proposed change on other documents in the organization and initiate the necessary changes.

USAGE

Many approved documents spend most of their active lives stored at the document library and their copies distributed so they are available at points of use.

This stage of the document lifecycle is commonly called 'distribution' implying the physical movement of documents from one place to the other. However, at this stage in their lives, documents are merely accessed and used, and are not always in distribution. In fact, in EDMSs, users are only given electronic access to documents and there is no physical distribution of documents. Document distribution is the fiber that enables and brings together the various document lifecycle stages. However, it is hard to call the distribution of documents a significant phase in a documents' life.

During the 'usage' phase, documents are accessed, read and used by users for their daily work. At times, documents are even amended lightly without a formal review. It is true that not all document changes will lead to comprehensive document reviews that result in new revisions.

Many companies allow minor changes to documents including correction of typographical errors, printing errors or change of originator's name without the need for a full review process. Documents with these types of errors can be corrected immediately, reprinted and distributed without a new revision code or management approval. The idea is that a full revision is not required as long as the content of the core document does not change. Other examples of minor changes are the renumbering of sections, renaming of titles, and clarifications that don't affect the intent or purpose of the document.

In some instances, even hand written amendments may be acceptable provided that all document copies are initiated and dated by the originator. This is a tradition that comes from the old days where documents had to be retyped all over again even to make the smallest changes. When making hand written changes, don't overwrite or scrabble. Any error must be crossed out so that the original remains legible. Scratched or whited out details put the integrity of the document in question.

However, some critical documents, particularly those which are transmitted externally to customers and suppliers, can't be changed without a formal review which will require a change in the document revision. The logic is that changes, even when they seem minor, may cause adverse quality issues and therefore the other party should be fully aware of the changes.

Consequently, to avoid any confusion about what changes can be made without a formal review, the document control procedure should provide clear guidance on how such changes should be dealt with. For example, the procedure needs to clearly describe and list what a 'minor document change' is and what is not. What document types (e.g. contracts, product specification, etc.) can (not) be modified without a proper review process? Should minor changes be communicated to other users? How? How many minor changes can be made to a document before a new revision is required?

As indicated at the beginning, original documents are always kept at the document library and users are not allowed to openly access them or to modify them without following the applicable review process. Instead, users are provided with copies of the documents so that the original is never lost or damaged. Certain authorized users may temporarily borrow the original copies from the document control center as long as the person borrowing the document is identified and documented.

An important aspect of document usage is access administration and information security. A good document administration ensures that documents are accessible only to the right users both in and outside the company, as needed. To make certain that each document is available to the right user, the organization needs to determine who needs which document and at what time. The document distribution matrix (DDM) is a comprehensive register with the names of the originators, reviewers, approvers and users for each document or document type. Originators and document controllers rely on the DDM to identify the proper reviewers and approvers, to issue documents accordingly, and to quickly remove outdated documents from circulation.

A key function of document control is keeping track of the issued documents. If you are the document controller or originator, you need to keep a record of people both inside and outside the organization to whom controlled documents were issued. Otherwise, you will have a hard time locating older revisions already in distribution and ensuring they are replaced by the latest ones when new revisions become available. In that sense, effective document distribution releases the latest revision of a document in a timely manner and removes the older revisions from circulation and use.

It is also important that the guidelines for the document security classifications are fully understood by the document controller, originator or user since confidentiality requirements may restrict document storage and distribution. Document controllers are expected to train users on how to work with confidential or proprietary information. They need to make sure that access to confidential documents is restricted to only those who need it.

Additionally, document controllers, together with the IT or information security department, need to make sure that documents are protected against cyber-attack, unauthorized access and change. Furthermore, document controllers are responsible for ensuring document back up is regularly maintained and that documents are protected against disasters such as flood and fire.

ARCHIVAL AND DISPOSAL

At the end of their lives, documents become obsolete and have to be archived and eventually discarded.

Perhaps the most common reason for document obsolescence is the release of a new revision which replaces an incorrect or outdated document rendering it obsolete. A document may also become obsolete when the product or activity it supports is discontinued or no longer carried out in the organization. Similarly, when projects are completed, documents that are not required to operate and maintain the outcome of the project (e.g. a wind farm) will have to be archived for future reference purposes.

When a new revision of a document is issued, the older one has to be removed from points of use. This ensures that errors, failures or hazards won't occur as a result of unintentionally using outdated documents. Accordingly, copies of the older revision will be collected and destroyed. The original will be clearly marked as obsolete and archived for reference and compliance purposes. This process needs to be carefully managed since documents can sometimes be distributed outside the company and it may be hard to easily retrieve them.

One way of facilitating the old document collection and disposal is to clearly mandate in the document control procedure that users need to return or destroy the obsolete document when they receive a new revision. If anyone needs to keep the obsolete document for their records, they can be asked to clearly mark it as an obsolete document and send to the document controller an acknowledgement that the old document has been replaced by the new one.

A more proactive and controlled way of collecting superseded documents from users makes use of what is known as a document retrieval form or recall notice. On the retrieval form, the document controller lists the number, revision and title of each just superseded document and issues the form to the users who are required to return the obsolete documents. The form can mention which documents replace the superseded ones so that users know what documents to use going forward. When issuing such a recall notice, the document controller is advised to keep a copy for his records.

Archived documents, in paper-based document environments, may be stamped 'OBSOLETE' or 'SUPERSEDED' on the cover page to clearly communicate the status of the document. EDMSs automatically archive old revisions and make only the latest accessible to users by default. Users can still access superseded documents but often at a different location within the system so that outdated documents are kept separate from live documents. In any case, it is advisable to clearly indicate on the cover page of the superseded document which document it has been replaced with. You can do the same in the new document to tell the reader what document it supersedes. This makes future referencing and understanding of the history of the document easier and the audit trail more complete.

Similarly, documents that are discontinued without a newer revision are updated to 'VOID,' 'CANCELLED' or similar status and given a new revision number and date of issue before they are archived. The new status and date allows users in the future to know exactly when the document was retired. Any obsolete document that needs to be reinstated must be reviewed, approved and released just like a new document.

Usually, especially in a paper-based document control operation, archiving involves removing documents from the current document control environment and preserving them in a separate 'inactive' documents facility that may not be immediately accessible to users. This allows for both low cost maintenance of the documents as well as less likelihood that quality will suffer as a result of obsolete document usage. In centralized EDMSs, however, a new document revision automatically replaces the old one which will no longer be available to users.

Note that archived documents need to be retained for a certain period of time before they can be destroyed. Retention period requirements are often determined by legal or organization-specific requirements, or in some cases by the potential historic or intrinsic value of the document. At end of the required retention period, archived documents can be destroyed or permanently deleted. For privacy, confidentiality and environmental reasons, document disposal must be carried out by an appropriate means given the nature, confidentiality and make-up of the document. Document retention and disposal overlaps with records management since obsolete documents are records. Therefore, it is a good idea to liaise with records management personnel in your organization to better understand detailed legal and procedural requirements for records archiving and disposal.

The following table summarizes the various tools you may need to manage the document control process.

	Document Lifecycle					
	Creation	Review	Approval	Usage	Archival + Disposal
Document Control Instrument	Document Control Procedure (Required for all document lifecycle)				
	Document Distribution Matrix (DDM)	Document Distribution Matrix (DDM)	Document Distribution Matrix (DDM)	Document Distribution Matrix (DDM)	Document Distribution Matrix (DDM)
	Document Creation Form	Document Change Request Form	Document Implementation Plan		Recall Notice
	Document Template	Document Review Form (EDMS)			
		Document Review Schedule			

Table 3.1: Documents control instruments and document lifecycle

Chapter 4

Document Control Governance

The purpose of this chapter is to give you an overview of what it takes to ensure an effective document control function for your organization.

Sometime I am asked: 'what else do you need other than 'IT' to control documents?' My answer usually starts with 'A lot more!' The creation and upkeep of an efficient document control system is the result of strong governance, planning, and monitoring, just like any other quality system.

Good document control governance requires a clear strategy that is consistent with the organization's vision and mission. The document control strategy must be supported by a sound plan and a robust document control process, which in turn must be accompanied by a comprehensive set of procedures, work instructions, forms and other instruments in order to deliver the intended results consistently.

This type of comprehensive governance structure may seem to be an overkill. It will be if you are a small firm with very limited document control activity. On the other hand, if you are a large company or project, you will likely benefit from such an arrangement. It will enable you to set a clear road map and to develop various tools that you will need to succeed in controlling documents.

DOCUMENT CONTROL STRATEGY AND PLAN

Effective document control requires an underlying strategy and a practical approach that are tailored to the needs of the organization that uses them. The strategy needs to be fully aligned with the company's vision, mission, key business processes, and quality policy, and should be made a part of the daily document management routine.

Common strategic issues in document control include:

- Innovation and delivery of smarter document control solutions
- Centralization or decentralization of document control functions in large organizations
- Insourcing or outsourcing of document control activities
- Minimizing physical (hardcopy) documents
- Determining where in the organization the document control department reports to
- Storage, archival and retention solutions and approaches
- Information security and disaster recovery models

Strategic issues involve decisions with far reaching consequences and often take a long time and significant investment to implement. This is, in fact, another reason for you to carefully develop your strategic moves and make sure they make complete sense.

Developing the strategy, therefore, should not be a copy-paste exercise from another company's strategy document. Instead, it has to be a philosophy developed with the overall strategy, goals, objectives and business drivers of your own company in mind. Business drivers for your company can be enhanced customer service, cost reduction, regulatory compliance or business continuity.

Similarly, while developing your strategy, you need to assess your current document control practices, strengths and weaknesses as a function. This will give you a realistic understanding of where you stand at the moment in terms of capabilities and opportunities, and where you need to be to help achieve your company's strategic objectives. A good definition of where you are now and where you want to be will enable you to develop a good strategy - your road map to delivering the document control service your organization needs.

Once clearly formulated, the strategy will serve as the basis to make a comprehensive plan that articulates your goals and important steps needed to realize your strategy. Part of your plan will be the design and implementation of your own fit-for-purpose document control process.

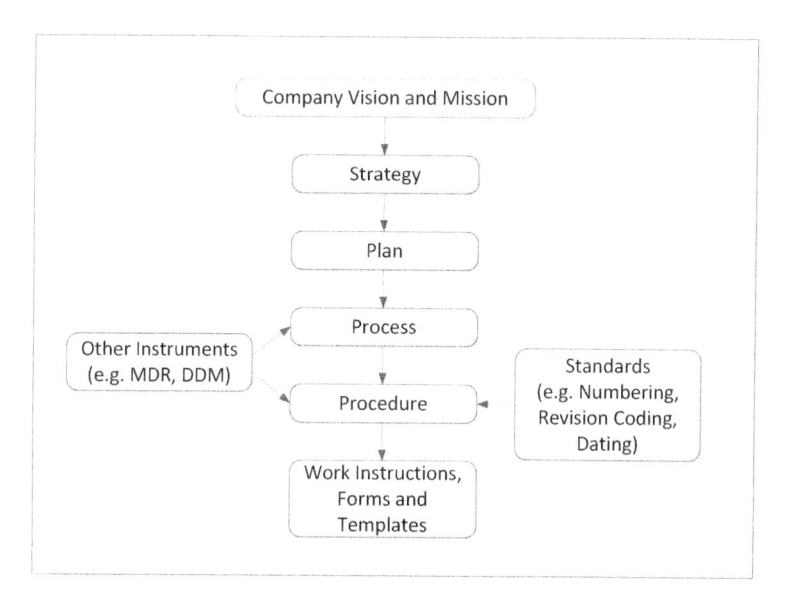

Figure 4.1: Elements of document control governance

In many instances the document control strategy and plan, and even the process may be already established and working, and you only have to improve them. Nevertheless, from time to time there may be decisions (e.g. implementing a new EDMS) that will require you to review your strategy, make new plans and adjust your document control process. Likewise, large projects (e.g. a construction project), as part of their overall control and quality assurance process, may require you to prepare a document control strategy and comprehensive plan detailing how you will handle different processes, and activities including document handover and quality assurance and control.

DOCUMENT CONTROL PROCESS AND PROCEDURE

The document control process includes activities and steps that make up document creation, review, approval, distribution, archival and disposal. It is at the heart of your document control and your success primarily depends on how good the process is.

The document control process must be clearly defined, documented and embedded in EDMS, procedures, and in other supporting instruments. The process also needs to be in line with your strategy or policy and should allow you to achieve your document control objectives.

To be effective, a document control process needs to support the organization's other business processes, culture and ways of working. It has to be flexible enough to allow the smooth flow of various documents to completion. A stringent process that requires all documents to go through the same series of activities (e.g. if approval and signatures for a form is expected from a senior manager as is normally required for a policy) can end up causing bottlenecks and frustration.

A procedure is usually a written document that describes what has to be done, why, how, by who, when, and where in order to achieve a desired result. It is meant to provide a high level sequence of actions that must be followed to correctly and consistently perform a task in support of an organization's process and policy directive.

A document control procedure is vital in both documenting your document management process and communicating it to your audience.

The procedure tells the document control participants how the process works and what is expected of them. Every document control function, regardless of company size, requires a procedure describing the process, roles and rules needed to ensure an effective and uniform document management practice.

A well-written and communicated document control procedure helps employees create and use the right documents for their work. It helps document controllers, writers, owners and users to manage documents in an agreed manner that meets the requirements of the organization and those of the relevant business and legal standards. It provides clear direction, contributes to better internal control and enhances compliance by helping to keep document control variations to a minimum.

Document control procedures commonly address the below issues.

- Planning, authorization, and establishment of new documents: who authorizes the planning and creation of new documents? How? Who should own the document? Who maintains the MDR?

- Preparation of new documents: who writes them? Who should be involved and how? Which template and graphic standards (e.g. company logo, colors) should be used for which kind of document? Where can templates be obtained?

- Dating, numbering and revision control convention: how should documents be dated, numbered and revised? What conventions should be used? What are the requirements for a new revision release? How are new document numbers issued and by who?

- Document review, approval and release: Who releases new documents and how? How will documents be reviewed and approved? What are the timelines? Who is involved and who is responsible for facilitating the document review? Who is responsible for approval? How will documents be signed?

- External documents management – how will external documents such as external regulations and standards be identified? How will document owners be identified? Who is responsible for the integration of such documents into the company's system? How will external documents be revised and how often? How will the document transmittal process with external parties work?

- Storage, access and distribution of documents: where should documents be stored? How should they be indexed? How will they be accessed? How will internal and external documents be distributed? How will physical documents be stored and distributed? Who will ensure that users always have the latest document at point of use? Are there any distribution restrictions because of document confidentiality?

- Amending and updating issued documents: how will documents be amended? Which changes can be made to a document without a new revision release? Who should make such changes? Which documents should be reviewed periodically? Who approves the changes? How will the change be communicated to affected users?

- Voiding, archiving and retention of outdated documents: how will obsolete documents be cancelled and removed from circulation? How, where and for how long should obsolete documents be stored?

- Reports and performance indicators: what kind of reports will be generated and how often? Which performance indicators will be used? By who?

- Quality Assurance and Quality Control: who is responsible for ensuring the quality and effectiveness of the document control process? What activities will be undertaken to do so? How often?

The document control procedure is often accompanied by supporting documents such as the document distribution matrix, list of document types and naming conventions, document numbering and revision coding scheme, instructions, forms and document templates. Some organizations go to extra length to prepare a qualification and training document to define the skills required of a person to review and approve documents. Some companies with a complex document control process write two or more procedures each addressing specific topics such as document review and approval, and document numbering and revising.

The bottom line is that document control procedures should be concise, but at the same time clear and detailed enough to provide the necessary direction as to how documents should be prepared and managed. They must be fully understood by the document controller and users need to understand the key processes around lifecycle management so that they can contribute to document creation and handling.

GOVERNING DOCUMENT CONTROL INSTRUMENTS

Over the years, document controllers have developed a number of instruments that are key in effectively controlling documents over their lifecycle. This section discusses two of them – the Master Document Register and Document Distribution Matrix.

Master Document Register

Master Document Register (MDR), also known as Documents Master Index, is the list of all documents you control – just like an inventory list. An up-to-date MDR is a vital aspect of every large document control environment. It tells you what and how many documents you have in your document control system.

A typical MDR shows every document's key identifying details such as the document number, document title, the latest revision number, and the document's date of issue. Other pieces of information such as completion status (i.e. draft, approved, etc.), the name of the originator or approver, location (e.g. URL to intranet), and anything else you find useful could also be included for each document in the MDR.

Every time a new document is created or an updated revision comes under the control process, these details about the document will be updated in the MDR. Therefore, for the document to be considered controlled, its identifying details must always match those on the MDR. If the document control system is audited, the master list is the source used to verify the control of individual documents. The MDR is important in providing you with an overview of your documents. It can also be used to report on the progress and status of your document set. Figure 4.2 provides a sample MDR.

One thing to remember is that you may want to control the MDR itself, and revise it each time a document is updated or a new one is created. In order to avoid repeated changes to the MDR, especially while working with paper-based registers, you can update it weekly or so. If you are using a spreadsheet-based MDR, updating will be easier, and so will be sorting and searching. You only need to be precise with your entries to facilitate exact searching and eventual export of data to other systems.

Doc No.	Title	Rev. No.	Rev. Date	Approver	Status
PRD-FIN-001	Credit Handling Procedure	02	06-12-2015	Jill Smith	Approved
POL-CNP-003	Purchasing Policy	05	23-11-2015	Jack Ian	Draft
FRM-HRM-008	Leave Request Form	03	13-03-2015	Ann Roy	Approved
WIN-PRO-012	Machine Set Up Instruction	07	28-07-2015	Emmy Jong	Approved

Figure 4.2: Sample Master Document Register (MDR)

Many EDMS also allow you to automatically generate an updated MDR anytime without the need for manual intervention. The EDMS database will be automatically updated whenever a new document is created or updated. This updated database will then be used to generate your up-to-date MDR. The MDR can be exported to a spreadsheet to enable easier document search and sorting.

Document Distribution Matrix (DDM)

Given the large volume of the documents that is often produced by companies, it is important for governance and quality assurance reasons to clearly assign document lifecycle responsibilities to individuals or departments. The tool that enables you to do that is known as the document distribution matrix (DDM).

The DDM is a table that identifies who is responsible for the creation, review and approval of the document. It gives you a visual reference to determine which documents are distributed to whom or to which department and for what purpose. Small teams can list all participants and indicate their roles as shown in Figure 4.3 below. Larger organizations can list roles such as write, review, approve and read (use) and list names of departments or participants. Distribution matrices are living documents, and are updated whenever there are changes in roles or the document list.

Document	Anthony (Director)	Bart (Production Manager)	Dugald (Technical Manager)	Richard (Procurement Manager)	Siva (Quality Manager)
Quality Manual	A*	R	R	R	A
Procurement Procedure	A	I	N/A	A	R
Production Schedule	I	A	R	I	R
Contracts	A	I	N/A	A	I
Product Specifications	I	A	R	R	A

*A= Approve R= Review I= For Information N/A= Not applicable, don't distribute

Figure 4.3: Sample Document Distribution Matrix (DDM)

DDMs can be 'generic' such as the one below listing only major document types (e.g. 'contracts', 'product specifications' etc.) or 'specific' with all documents listed by title and identification number. The latter is more manageable if all documents are predetermined and limited in number.

Computerized spreadsheet tools, such as Excel, are great tools for creating a document distribution matrix. You can also use any software that allows you to create tables. If your organization is small, you may be able to draw your matrix by hand. Large organizations with EDMS have their distribution matrix embedded in the system and only need to be populated with document details and names of participants.

Some companies keep the distribution matrix for each document on the document itself. While this practice puts the distribution of the documents at the reader's finger tips, it causes significant administrative work and is not effective. For instance, the document may need to go through a whole new review and approval cycle if a department or a person has to be added to the DDM.

DOCUMENT CONTROL ORGANIZATION

There is considerable debate about where in the organization, document control should be. This may sound like a silly discussion but positioning the document control in the right part of the organization can make the difference between an excellent and flexible service and a mediocre one. This is a strategic issue that needs to be carefully determined, especially if you are setting up a new document control function.

Many people feel document control should be part of the Quality Assurance and Control team. Others believe that document controllers should report to engineering. If you ask projects, they will probably tell you that document control is best placed under Project Services (Control), which provides support to projects in areas of finance, risk management and reporting. Other individuals in large organizations would say that document control should be decentralized where each department has its own document control function.

The role of the document control function depends on the unique circumstances of the organization. It is important for the document control authority to be placed with the department that is responsible for creating and using documents. If it is a manufacturing plant, it is probably appropriate for document control to be part of the manufacturing team. If you are on a design and construction project, then perhaps it is more appropriate to attach document control to the engineering department. There is no one right answer that serves all situations best. It all depends on how well you want the document control function to support your key processes.

Regardless of the location of document control, it is important to remember that controlling documents is the responsibility of all employees. They must all understand the purpose of document control and how to control and work with documents in accordance with the designated processes and procedures.

THE ROLE OF THE DOCUMENT CONTROLLER

Document control is a vital function that is part of the quality management system. The document controller, being an important contributor to quality, plays a key role in ensuring that the document management process works as envisioned.

The document controller's job is to manage documents to a required degree of reliability for security, revision, visibility, availability, and most importantly auditability. The responsibilities of document controllers may vary with the industry and may depend on the document management methods that are used. They look after a wide range of activities including facilitation of document flow, assurance of the documents' safety and security, training and coaching of staff as well as the design, set up and management of the document control process

Document controllers are responsible for registering, storing, cataloguing, distributing, tracking, receiving, retrieving and archiving documents. They ensure the integrity of documents and registers by checking the accuracy of the data about the documents and their storage. Document controllers also play a key role in the quality assurance of documents. They check documents for typographical errors, appropriate use of templates, missing parts and other errors before the documents are distributed for use.

Depending on the document control processes in place, document controllers are required to track pending documents and monitor deadlines by designing and generating periodic document control progress reports. They use reports and metrics to monitor the health of the document control process and to contribute to project or departmental meetings.

Senior document controllers set up document control processes and the required governance structure. They are involved in the selection, acquisition, and implementation of EDMS and office filing systems. They lead and coach junior document controllers.

Senior document controllers also train staff on how to write documents and efficiently use available document management systems. They write and promote document control procedures, EDMS user guides, instructions and other documents required to support the document control process. They also work with their counterparts in the client's or contractor's organization to ensure the quality and timely delivery of documents, such as in the case of projects.

In order to effectively carry out these varied responsibilities, document controllers require a number of skills and experiences.

They must be detail-oriented and able to work with a high volume of documents in a fast-paced and dynamic work environment. They also need to be highly organized and process-oriented.

Document control staff must also be customer-focused since the document control function is essentially a support department with both internal and external customers. Strong oral and written communication and interpersonal skills are essential for document controllers in order to enable them to interact well with people at all levels of the organization.

Document controllers are also expected to work both independently and in a team environment. They have to be proactive, flexible, and be able to prioritize. Understanding top priorities, focusing on a task and following it through under pressure are important skills for document controllers. They also need to be self-auditing and need to have high quality standards. In a construction or project environment, familiarity with project lifecycle, technical documents and drawings are essential for the document controller.

Companies are expected to give document controllers clear responsibilities, equivalent authority, necessary training and the required resources needed for a successful document control.

Chapter 5

Document and Revision Numbering

The numbering of documents appears to be straightforward. However, it can be a potentially tricky business with far reaching consequences. The practice of document numbering varies from one organization to another, and is widely debated by practitioners. Unfortunately, many organizations make poor decisions which negatively impact business performance.

Most of the debate on document numbering schemes comes from the lack of understanding on the potential complexity of document control systems. There are significant differences in the numbering needs of a 10-man business where only two people write documents, and a $10-billion project in which multiple companies with hundreds of document originators collaborate.

The main purpose of numbering documents is to uniquely identify them. Once assigned to a document, a document number never changes (unless absolutely required such as in order to accommodate a new critical business requirement) and is never duplicated or given to another document. It remains unchanged throughout the life of that document, regardless of approval status or change in revision.

Document numbers are similar to your social security number. Your name (for documents that is equivalent to document title), address (physical or electronic storage address for documents), physical descriptions (template and even content for documents) and other details may help to identify you. However, these details are likely to change over time. The very unique detail about you from a public administration perspective is your social security number which is unlikely to change.

Just like your personal administrative record is linked to your social security number, the history of documents is attached to their document number. If you don't have a social security number, from an administrative point of view, you don't really exist. The same is true for documents. You can't control a document that is not numbered. It won't show up on your MDR, and what is not on your MDR is not in your document control scope. For documents, 'to be' is to be numbered.

However, that is not the only use of document numbers. In addition to serving as a means of unique identification, document numbers allow you to logically organize, search, retrieve and recognize documents quicker.

As an example, assume that you come across a document numbered 'QP-PRD-007.' You can easily guess that this is a quality procedure (QP) for the production (PRD) department. Alternatively, if you know the document number you can more easily browse and locate the document, especially if you are operating a traditional paper-based document library. Even in the EDMS world, many systems rely on the clues in the document number to store and retrieve documents.

Document numbers also make document cross referencing easier and more reliable. It is often easier to refer to another document by just mentioning the document number instead of the title. This is because document numbers are unique and usually shorter than titles.

CONSIDERATIONS IN DOCUMENT NUMBERING DESIGN

What sort of document numbering scheme should you use? I would start by asking: do you really need to number your documents?

The short answer is yes, if you work with a reasonably large number of documents or if there is a regulation or standard that requires you to number your documents. On the other hand, if you are a small business with four or five document users, and just 10 or 15 documents exclusively used internally then you can probably manage without document numbers. You can just give each document a good title and you should be fine. However, that does not mean you don't have to control your documents. You will still need to assign clear responsibilities for document writing, review, and approval among your team and undertake important document control activities.

What are the important considerations that you need to take into account while developing a fit-for-purpose document numbering system?

Make the numbering serve your needs

There are many ways to number your documents. There is no one best way to do it. Various industries and businesses have different requirements for numbering. Therefore, when thinking about how to label and control documents, you should think about how you expect your users to search for, retrieve and use the documents. Whatever your business needs, they should be reflected in your document number. Therefore, you should keep the numbering as simple as possible to make it work for you.

The first step is to clearly identify your organization's document numbering needs. Do you want your numbering to reflect the quality management system triangle (policy, procedure, instruction and forms) or the departmental structure of your organization? Is year of publication of the document important enough for you to embed it in the document number? Or do you plan to use dead simple sequential numbers and manage document storage and retrieval using metadata?

Don't fall into the trap of developing a fancy, but complex, confusing and awkward numbering scheme that captures unnecessary details and makes maintenance burdensome. Failing to incorporate the needs of your business will make document identification and retrieval difficult for users and create additional work for document controllers.

Having said that, if you are an organization that operates complex facilities such as a refinery or large factory, you might need two document numbering scheme. The first is for your non-engineering and company-wide documents such as human resources or procurement policy that are classified across major departments. The second scheme will be for your design and engineering documents which are often organized based on the physical breakdown of your factory (i.e. plants and process units). As a result, while some EDMS may accommodate both sets of documents, it may be very hard to come up with a single numbering scheme that will work well for both general administrative and facilities-related technical documents.

Design it to last

The ideal document number scheme should serve you well indefinitely without any change to it. Changes to document numbering scheme are often disruptive to business since they cause confusion and require money and time to implement. Therefore, while designing your scheme, identify organizational or document numbering aspects that may change in the future and ensure they won't affect your numbering system.

The first issue that comes to mind is the possibility of running out of document numbers. Let us say that you decided to use a numbering structure and number your first maintenance work instruction 'WI-MNT-01.' Before you know it, you have to write the hundredth maintenance work instruction. How would you number that? Perhaps you have to introduce a third digit (i.e. WI-MNT-101) which will create inconsistency in your numbering or require you to renumber all of your other documents.

To avoid that, while designing your documents, obtain a good estimate of how many documents are expected in each major category. Find out if the company has plans to expand or grow which will affect your document numbering scheme. It is also important to determine if there are legacy documents (i.e. documents currently stored in another system but which need to be brought into your document library) which you are not aware of but need to be given new numbers and be part of the new document control center.

It is important to refrain from using codes that may change in the future. It is common, for instance, to add department codes in document numbers. In principle, that is not a problem unless your company is re-organized. Company reorganizations often abolish and merge existing departments or even create new ones. These changes will affect your numbering, and might force you to redesign your numbering scheme and re-number all of your documents.

Similarly, some organizations chose to link their numbering back to a clause number of an international standard such as ISO 9001. That is, in reference to clause 4.17, the document number for a quality procedure might be '4.17-QP-PRD-007'. The rationale behind this numbering is to enable users to immediately identify which clause of the standard the document satisfies. If you are auditing against specific clauses of the standard, you can easily identify the ones that apply to it from hundred other documents. This numbering approach may work perfectly fine, but the vulnerability is that you are bound to re-number all such documents if the next revision of the standard has a different number for that specific clause. An example is if the new standard clause 4.17 becomes clause 5.17. In that case, all documents will have to be re-numbered or you risk creating confusion.

Another numbering consideration has to do with project-related documents which are handed over at the completion of the project to an owner-operator organization that will run the services or facilities created by the project. The project and the owner-operator organization often may have different numbering systems, because they could be organized differently. These differences in document numbering often require the renumbering of project documents before they are handed over to the owner-operator at the end of the project.

To avoid the renumbering of documents, as the client's document controller, first see if the receiving organization's document numbering system is already established and if it can be used for your project. However, in many cases, projects and operating assets have different numbering needs, and at times the receiving organization may not yet even exist. The latter is particularly true for the design and construction of new facilities where the start of the project is really the beginning of everything. In such cases, there is very little you can do apart from making sure that document templates have an extra space to add the owner-operating company's document numbers at project completion. You could also add to each of the project document, a cover page containing the operator's new applicable document number, company logo and other necessary details.

Use familiar codes for numbering

If you decide to use alpha-numeric document numbers, make sure you use codes that users are familiar with. For example, many people will immediately recognize 'QM' as quality management. But if you name it '01' instead, it will be less clear. Make sure that the numbering abbreviations for departments, processes, etc. are easily recognizable and at the same time not too similar to each other to create confusion. If your documents are expected to be shared with external parties, you might want to consider using an abbreviation at the start of the number that represents the name of your company (e.g. ABC-QM-0001).

It is always a good idea to test your new numbering scheme with real users and receive their feedback. This exercise not only gives you opportunities to improve your numbering but also helps you create a sense of ownership among the users.

Ensure the scheme is documented and communicated to users

Many organizations find it useful to write a document numbering instruction, which can be part of their document control procedure or a separate document. This ensures that all users understand how documents are numbered and why. In the numbering instruction, you can describe how users can obtain document numbers for their new documents. You can also include document revision coding instructions in the same document. Keep your document numbering procedure clear, concise and complete like any other good procedure.

Administer numbers centrally

Since the same document number should never be used on two different documents, the creation and distribution of document numbers should be centrally administered. Many organizations assign the responsibility of issuing new document numbers to the document controller. If you are in a large organization where significant number of new documents are created, you can consider using a document number request form (Figure 5.1). The form can be a spreadsheet that enables the requester to provide the details that will enable the document controller to generate the right number for the specific document type. Once completed, the form can be emailed to the document controller who will generate the next available number for that specific document, register it in the system and send the number to the requester.

People can also be allowed to generate numbers using automated EDMS services. However, assurance needs to be put in place to make sure that users don't generate numbers they won't use. Similarly, projects partnering with two or more contractor companies sometime issue document numbers in 'blocks' (e.g. document numbers 1 to 100 to contractor A, and 101 to 200 to contractor B) so that the contractors don't have to send repeated number requests for each new document. In this case, ensure that the document numbers issued to the different parties are not duplicated and no two parties have the same document number.

Document Number Request Form	
Document Title:	
Department:	
Document Type:	
Originator Name:	
Date:	

Figure 5.1: Example document number request form

ALTERNATIVE DOCUMENT NUMBERING SCHEMES

Bear in mind that there is no one numbering scheme that works best in all situations. A good numbering scheme can be anything as long as it helps you uniquely identify and retrieve your documents quickly. Below are some commonly used numbering schemes.

Intelligent vs non-intelligent document numbers

Document numbers can be either 'intelligent' or 'non-intelligent'. Non-intelligent document numbers are simple numbering methods such as '14525' that don't say anything about the nature or content of the document. As you will soon read, such numbers have their own advantages and can be effectively used in certain circumstances.

In contrast, document numbers can be designed to tell the reader more about the document. Such numbers are called 'intelligent.' Intelligent document numbers contain predefined static values such as acronyms representing document types, departments or units the document belongs to, or other details that have to do with the content of the document. The number 'QP-PRD-007' that we looked at earlier is a good example.

Intelligent numbering seems to be more informative and helps to identify documents better, especially in a paper based document control environment. It helps you to logically organize your documents based on location, department, product, year of writing, etc. This forces you to consistently store a particular document in the right location and enables other people to find it easily. There is, however, a strong argument against the use of intelligent numbering which we will discuss shortly.

```
              /\
             /  \
            /    \
           / Quality Manual \
          /                  \
         /    Procedures      \
        /                      \
       /    Work Instructions   \
      /                          \
     /          Forms             \
    /_____\
    |      Reference Documents     |
```

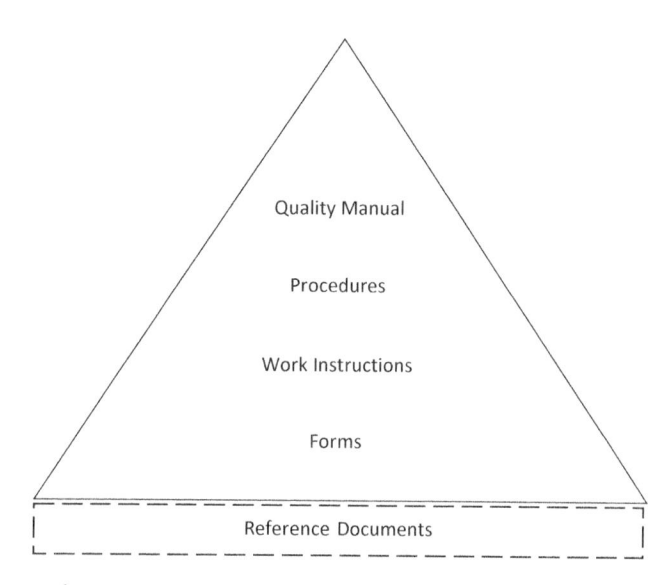

Figure 5.2: Quality Management System triangle

Numbering scheme for Quality Management documents

A common way of organizing quality management related documents is using the quality management system triangle (see Figure 5.2). This hierarchy includes quality policy or manual at the highest level followed by procedures, work instructions and forms. Reference documents such as a controlled list of machinery part suppliers which are deemed part of the quality management system can be added at the bottom of the hierarchy to provide a more complete picture and to control all documents centrally. Generally, as you go down the hierarchy, the number of documents at each level increases.

A simple numbering scheme in this situation categorizes documents at each level of the triangle and numbers them sequentially. Here is an example.

Document Control

Level	Sample Document Number	Notes
Level 1	QM-0001	QM for Quality manual or policy, 0001 represents the first document of its kind
Level 2	PR-0003	PR for Procedure
Level 3	WI-0007	WI for work instruction
Level 4	FM-0011	FM for form
Level 5	RF-0014	RF for reference document

Table 5.1: Sample document numbering scheme

This numbering can be hard to use if your organization decides to combine a manual with related procedures and instructions together to create a single document. Labelling such document a 'manual' could solve the problem provided that you also communicate the nature of the document well.

As Table 5.2 shows, a twist to the above numbering scheme enables the traceability of documents (e.g. a procedure) back to higher level documents (e.g. a quality manual) in the document hierarchy. This is made possible by adding, for example, the document number of the manual at the back of the number of the procedure.

Level	Sample Document Number	Notes
Level 1	QM-0001	QM for Quality manual or policy
Level 2	PR-0003- QM-0001	Procedure that is based on the QM-0001
Level 3	WI-0007-PR-0003	Work instruction to assist PR-0003
Level 4	FM-0011-WI-0007	Form to enable WI-0007
Level 5	RF-0014-PR-0003	Reference document that is used together with PR-0003

Table 5.2: Sample document numbering scheme with traceability

On the other hand, if you feel you have multiple departments in your organization and adding a departmental code makes document retrieval quicker, you can think of a numbering arrangement in Table 5.3.

Level	Sample Document Number	Notes
Level 1	QM-ENG-0001	Quality manual for the (ENG) Engineering Department
Level 2	PR-MNT-0003	A Procedure for the maintenance department
Level 3	WI-PRD-0007	Work instruction for the production department
Level 4	FM-DCM-0011	Form for document control department
Level 5	RF-MKT-0014	Reference document used by the marketing unit

Table 5.3: Sample document numbering scheme with department codes

You can also introduce an additional code, say 'MST' (machine set up), next to 'PRD' if you want to organize your documents down to specific processes in a department. In this case, the document number may become 'WI-PRD-MST-0001'. This allows you to more specifically give an indication of what process the work instruction relates to.

Whatever numbering that you come up with, remember to keep it simple, consistent and aligned with your company's requirements.

Project or product based numbering

It could sometimes be advantageous to organize your documents around specific products or projects. This is particularly useful if you have more than one major product or project and you want to clearly identify which product or project each document belongs to. In this case, the document number may start with an alpha-numeric code that represents the project or product.

As an example, large projects, especially in construction, are carried out by clients in collaboration with construction contractor companies and their sub-contractors and suppliers. This creates a complex numbering scenario where document numbers have to reflect not only the structure of the project or the owner of the facility being built, but also the numbering philosophy of the document originator (e.g. a design contractor).

Project document numbers often indicate the name of the project, the originator of the document (e.g. client, contractor or vendor), department or discipline, part of the facilities concerned (e.g. plant, unit), and may go into further detail, and may even have a code to indicate what sort of document it is (e.g. drawing, datasheet, etc.).

An interesting aspect is that some document numbers may change as documents exchange ownership from one party to the other. For instance, a drawing developed by a design contractor may have a number based on the design contractor's internal numbering system. When the drawing is signed-off and transferred to the client's document control, it will be given a new number based on the client's own numbering plan.

Furthermore, as described earlier, some completed projects hand over their documents to another company that will operate the newly constructed facilities. If the client's project and new operator's document numbering systems are not the same, then a cover page containing the operator's document number is added to each project document to override the project document number and enable good document control by the operator.

It is also important to note that what is known as sheet number can be part of a project or product document number. For example, if a design drawing represents a continuation from one sheet to another and as a result it is necessary for the subsequent drawing to possess the same document number as the previous drawing, sheet numbers (e.g. ABC-ENG-CVL-0001-000) will be used at the end of the drawing number. Each additional sheet will be numbered 001, 002 etc., but with the same document number. Similarly, sheet numbers can be applied to large documents that need to be broken down for the purposes of practicality.

Metadata as document numbering

Modern EDMS systems use metadata to facilitate document storage and retrieval. Metadata are pieces of information about a particular document. For instance, in order to release a new document in EDMS, you will need to fill in the name of the originator, the document title, revision number, date of issue, document type, document status, transmittal number, key words and, of course, document number among other details. All of these details later enable you to search for the document by using the EDMS's search engine, much like you would use key words to search for content on Google.

Metadata can be used together with a complex document numbering scheme. It is also possible to use very simple sequential document numbers and let the metadata do the document retrieval for you in the EDMS. This is increasingly popular since many organizations with a high volume of documents completely switch to electronic document control systems.

As an example, suppose you just developed a new form that belongs to the human resources department and supports recruitment process based on procedure Y and work instruction Z. If we were to come up with a number for this form in a way to capture all of these details, it will be rather complex. What metadata potentially allows you to do in this case, is to just assign the next available number (e.g. 000047) to the form and capture the rest of the details as metadata in the EDMS as you upload the form. This creates a form with a simple document number but with a number of key words that will enable the users to easily search and find the form. If the function is supported by your EDMS, a user who wants to find this form only has to type 'recruitment form' and the EDMS will list all of the forms with their titles.

With the help of your EDMS's reporting services, metadata fields are reportable giving you great flexibility to generate a variety of reports.

The use of sequential document numbering based on metadata is particularly helpful if, for instance, departments merge or if you inherit documents from a legacy or paper-based system with a different numbering system. In such cases, as long as the document numbers remain unique, you only need to update the metadata behind each document to reflect the required changes. This saves you considerable effort that would otherwise be required to re-number all documents.

In this sense, metadata almost makes document numbering irrelevant since users can continue to search and find their documents based on metadata. It is possible that if you have a metadata enabled EDMS, you don't even need to number your documents at all.

The reality, however, is that you usually need document numbers not only to store and retrieve documents in EDMS but also to refer to documents precisely by their numbers in your internal and external communication.

There may also be a document control scenario where you will be better off with good old document numbering. Imagine that you work in a factory that suddenly experiences an emergency followed by a complete power failure. To respond to the unexpected situation, you, the authorized manager, need to urgently find the emergency response procedure. But no power means that the metadata-driven and computer-based EDMS is not working, and you need to find the printed copy of the document stored in the physical library. Chances are the library contains many or even thousands of other documents, all numbered sequentially without any logical grouping. That is when you realize that you are in trouble!

DOCUMENT REVISION NUMBERING

Document revisions

It is very important to clarify what document revision and version really mean. These two terms may mean two different things depending on the nature of your documents and how you decide to control them.

A version can mean a document that is essentially the same in content as another, but may be targeted for a different user group. Take the example of two versions of a procedure, one in English and the other in Spanish. Versions can be cars of the same model but with different colors. Logically numbering documents along with their multiple versions will help in their retrieval and their management over their lifecycle.

In the computerized world of document writing, a version can also mean the specific identifying number given to an electronic document file every time it is edited and saved. This allows for an audit trail of the changes made to a document during its writing as the software stores and provides users access to the distinct versions of the document saved at different points in time.

On the other hand, a revision represents a document and its content on a certain day and time. A latest revision of a document contains the most up-to-date content and therefore replaces the previously issued revisions of the same document.

Controlled documents, in addition to unique numbers, require a revision number. While document revision numbers may not be unique to a document, their primary purpose is to help users identify the latest revision of the document. Without the revision code, users will have difficulty telling which of the two or more copies of a document is the most recent.

Users often have old and new revisions of the same document. An example could be a copy that was printed out a month ago and one that was newly released. In such cases, the documents need to have something that identifies the latest revision. Otherwise, the wrong document will potentially be used, leading to quality problems.

In EDMS, document revision control is one of the most critical functions because it ensures that users always have access to the most current revision of the document. Revision control prevents documents from being overwritten or deleted in the EDMS as they are updated and a new revision is made available. This is made possible by giving the new document a new revision number, essentially making it the latest and most valuable document available to users. All previous revisions of the document will be maintained by the system in the event that they are required for future reference.

Similar to document numbering, it is important to note that there is no rule or one best way of coding for document revision. But there is an important question: when do you need to update the revision of a document?

A new revision of a document is an absolute requirement if the content of the document changes, requiring users to do things differently. It is unclear whether you need to release a new revision of the document when you are only making minor changes. The answer depends on a number of factors.

Companies that utilize paper-based documentation are in a better position to make minor changes such as the correction of spelling errors or rewording statements for clarity without review and releasing the next revision of the document. This can be done by the document owner by simply putting their initials against the change.

On the other hand, if the company uses an EDMS, documents are most likely locked against editing. In principle, an EDMS must force the issue of a new document revision number every time a document is replaced by a new one. However, depending on the quality risk involved, the security feature of EDMSs may be relaxed so that minor changes can be made to documents without a formal review and approval.

From an administrative and control perspective, in some industries documents are so critical to quality and safety you may not be allowed to modify them at all in any form or shape without a formal review process. In this case, any change to a document, whatever it is, means a new revision. On the other hand, if the document is less critical to the business and you are working with paper documents or a more open EDMS system, you may want to be able to make small changes to your documents without a new revision. This is especially useful if the review and approval of a document involves many people or takes too much time.

In summary, there is no one best way to control your documents. The approach that helps you achieve your business objectives is the right approach. Whatever revision rules you make and follow, ensure they are clearly captured in your document control procedure and communicated to users.

Alternative ways to revision coding

There are many different ways to number the revision of your documents. Three common ways that document revision is coded are presented below.

Date of issue

Including the issue date on the document is one way to help users identify the latest document. In order to include the date in a document it is useful to print it on the cover page and header or footer of every other page of the document. That helps you to identify the revision of each page of a printed document. You also have the option of including the date in the document number. For example, the number WI-PRO-0001-24-08-15 lets you know that the document was released on the 24th of August.

Some companies, on the other hand, choose automated time stamping on each document whenever it is printed for use instead of including the date in the document when it is first released. This might work fine but it may also leave the reader confused when they are faced with copies of the same document printed on different dates.

Revision number

Including a revision number in addition to date of issue in your documents, gives you additional advantages. For example, the date alone does not tell you how many times the document has been updated, unless you keep a revision history on each document.

A revision number can be an important metadata that you can use to generate reports. For instance, do you have any document that has been updated many times (say three or more times) in the past year? By which departments? You may need to look closely at the processes and departments behind these documents to see what you can do to help.

Some companies use decimal points to indicate revision status. For example, the revision number 1.1 says a minor revision has been released since the first major release of the document. Other organizations use the same method to differentiate between draft and approved documents. Whole numbers such as 1.0 or 2.0 represent approved revisions while 1.3 shows the document is in draft mode and under review. When this document is approved, the revision number changes to 2.0 to reflect the document status.

Similarly, you can use numbers and letters or a combination of the two to indicate revision and document status. A simple scheme could be 1R for the first review, 2R for the second review and 3A if the document is approved the next time.

In addition to revision numbers, some companies use issue numbers. The revision number is used to reflect documents updated as a result of minor changes. Following major documentation updates (e.g. change in quality vision, objective, organizational structure or upgrade to a new quality standard) or the completion of the highest number of minor changes prescribed by the document control procedure often lead to the next document issue. If the threshold limit is 20 for making revision to a document without updating the issue number, the 21st revision would lead to the next issue. For example, from Issue 01 Revision 20 to Issue 02 Revision 00. The revision number is often reset following a new document issue as shown in the example.

Chapter 6

Document Templates

A template is a ready-made style and content guide for a document showing what a completed document should look like. It is a starting point for creating new documents and is an important element of the document quality assurance effort.

A template may contain many elements such as the company logo, header and footer, automated table of contents, placeholder text, dictionaries, auto-text entries, toolbars and macros in addition to fonts, formatting styles and coloring. Every organization that produces a large volume of documentation is advised to have a set of standard document templates. For example, many companies have templates for word documents, spreadsheets and drawings which all document writers are expected to use. Other companies also use more specialized templates to write specifications, procedures, and process descriptions.

The effective and efficient use of documents partly depends on the standardized use of templates. Therefore, all document templates needs to be numbered, controlled and distributed to users just like any other controlled documents.

WHY USE TEMPLATES

Consistent and comprehensive information capture

The purpose of having templates is to ensure consistency in the way that information is captured and presented across an organization.

The idea is that any new document made using a template will contain the same underlying datasets, fields, formatting, layout and other features as the template document. This helps you to create documents that not only have a similar look and feel, but also the professional quality that meets your audience's expectations, even when you are new to document writing. Documents that are based on well-designed templates make a good impression on stakeholders, and good impressions can have a lasting and beneficial impact on your business. Furthermore, when you use a template, you are much less likely to miss important aspects of the document that needs to be incorporated. This is because the headers and text of the template remind you of all the key topics that you need to consider.

From document control point of view, templates also play a key role in helping capture details required to initiate and manage the document control process. For example, a typical word document template will have writing space for the document number, title, revision number, date of issue, names of the originator, reviewer and approver.

Improved productivity and collaboration

For the document originator, the biggest advantage of having templates is the time that can be saved by using them. Templates jumpstart document writing by providing structure, layout and even content.

Built-in parts such as chapter and section headers not only tell you what information to include in the document, but also help you avoid non-stop arguments about what a document should include and how it should be organized. That means less confusion, rework and frustration.

Standard and automated layout and formatting also enable you to focus on the content of the document and leave the formatting to the template. Some templates even have placeholder text (auto-text) which you can re-use with minimum change. Similarly, clever document templates also help you automate some elements of the document writing. For example, a Microsoft Word document can be designed to allow the automated preparation of table of contents or to help you choose pre-designed formats of titles and text so you don't have to do it every time.

Time is also saved when you read through a document written using a template you are familiar with. Your familiarity with the parts of the template allows you to more easily spot the information you want. This is especially important in a work environment such as projects where two or more document writers or companies work together. In the same way, unique template features such as company logos help readers to quickly identify documents, especially in work environments where you have documents from multiple companies.

TEMPLATE PARTS

It is essential to point out that there is no one right way of designing templates. It all depends on the specific needs of your company.

For example, administrative workers don't mind including elaborate revision history, and even a brief summary on the cover page of a policy document. On the other hand, users on the production floor may prefer to have these details minimized or kept at the back of the document since they want to get to the main details quickly.

In this section, you will read about the different parts of a sample word document template.

Cover page

The cover page of a word document can have a number of parts including company name and logo, revision record table, signatures and even a short abstract.

The need for control gives templates distinctive features such as a title, document number, document type, revision code, document status (reason for issue), date of issue or approval, names of originator, reviewers and approvers, and their approval signature. These are all details commonly kept on the cover page and required for identification, tracking and quality assurance of the document from inception to its end of life.

Details such as the document revision number, status and names of reviewers and approvers, which change or are likely to change from one revision to the other, can be organized into the 'revision record' table. Every time the document is updated and a new revision is issued, the latest details will be shown in a new row in the table. The revision record table can also be used to keep track of changes made to the document. You can add a 'changes' column to the revision record table to identify the parts or pages of the document that are modified in the latest revision. This allows readers to quickly know what was changed without reading the whole document. If you are, however, dealing with a large document that often goes through many changes then you can keep a separate 'change control table' on the next page or as an attachment to the document. This allows you to limit the amount of text written on the cover page. Other more permanent details such as the document number and title can be written in capital and bold face letters for easier identification by users.

Other details that you may see on the cover page are the name of the project (if it is a project document), the security classification of the document (confidential, restricted, public), page number (which is often expressed as 'Page 1 of 15' to indicate the size of the document) and a disclaimer on copyright.

	DOCUMENT NUMBER:	
XYZ Inc	**ABC-XX-YYY-000-0000**	
	DOCUMENT TITLE	
	INFORMATION SECURITY CLASSIFICATION:	
	(CONFIDENTIAL/RESTRICTED)	Page 1 of ----

ABSTRACT

This document describes....

Revision Record
Write initial and surname in full in the last three columns. Signatures not required in this page

01R	01-Jan-2015	Issued for Review	(Name)	(Name)	(Name)
Rev	**Date**	**Document Status**	**Originator**	**Reviewer(s)**	**Approver(s)**

Figure 6.1: Sample cover page for a word document

Header and footer

Headers and footers are often kept on all pages of the document except the cover page.

The header or footer repeats the title of the document, its number, revision code, document status and release date on each page of the document. If your document is to be shared externally with other companies, you might consider including the name of your company or project in the header or footer.

The reason that such document identifying details are kept in the header or footer is to help the reader find the master copy of the document if, for example, the cover page of the document is misplaced. Sometimes different document revisions become mixed up and the only way to determine the page is to look at document number, revision code and status contained in the header or footer. You have to decide whether to keep such details in the header or footer while designing your template. Here is an example header.

| ABC INC. SPECIFICATION: PRODUCT XYZ | 15-JAN-2015 | Rev 03 Approved | Page 5 of 18 |

Figure 6.2: Sample header for a document

Other parts

The typical word document template contains many other parts. These include table of contents, executive summary, placeholder text and tables, pre-numbered chapters and sub-sections.

Templates may also include standard formats for tables, process (swim-lane) diagrams and other illustrations. Standard fonts enable you to swiftly format text according to the set standard without bothering to choose font type and size. All of these features can be created using a standard Microsoft Word.

CREATING AND USING DOCUMENT TEMPLATES

Template creation

A good template is one that is fit-for-purpose and easy to edit and organize ideas into.

It contains, when necessary, filler text or "placeholders" to show font selections, sizes and alignment of text and may even provide brief instructions to guide the document writer. It also helps organize content in such a way that readers will find what they are looking for easily.

A well-thought-out template also has all of the unique details that enable effective document identification and control (e.g. document title, number, revision, so on), and works with a wide range of software platforms, versions, and widely available fonts.

The first question to answer before creating a document template is: is there an existing template that serves your purpose? It is important to note that, in some situations, your templates may be provided by the client and you don't need to create one yourself. This is particularly true if you are providing services (e.g. engineering design) or goods (e.g. printing) to other companies. But if the answer to the above question is 'no', then you probably need to design your own template.

Before starting the actual template design, I always find it useful to look around on the Internet for a template that I can use as a starting point. There are a number of sites that provide different types of free templates intended for various purposes. Some quick research can give you many ideas and tips on the latest template design trends.

You can also look into your publishing computer programs to see what is available. Many word processing and desktop publishing software products provide free document templates. While these templates will give you a good start, they will often require some work, for instance, embedding your company name, logo, document number etc..

Depending on your familiarity with your publishing software, you may be able to design quality templates from scratch.

An important step in creating a template is understanding the template's specific purpose and how it will be used. Some companies have templates for each kind of document such as policies, procedures, instructions etc. Others would like to create fewer templates (e.g. template for Word Documents, Spreadsheets, etc.) that provide general guidelines enabling the use of the template for more than one kind of document.

When the expected purpose and use of the templates is clear, you can start designing each template with input from your stakeholders. It is important to circulate each template for comments among expected users. Remember that your template will only be successful if its prospective users find it easy to use and helpful. Involving key users of the templates during the design stage, helps you to obtain valuable feedback which you can use to build a lasting document template.

Building lasting templates the first time and delaying template updates as long as possible provide a number of benefits. First, many template changes distract users since they have to get used to the alterations and apply the new template to existing documents that are updated and released. Secondly, updating templates means the templates of newer documents will have a different look and feel from those of older documents, unless the new template is applied to all existing documents. Depending on how frequent and drastic these templates changes are, the document library may become a mixed bag of document templates where two or more documents from different points in time look entirely different.

From a technological perspective, it is important to keep in mind factors such as the software version (release), file type (.docx, .dwg, etc), fonts and so on while designing electronic templates. These technological aspects may restrict the templates usability as a result of incompatibility between different software versions or fonts.

Once your template is reviewed, and your key stakeholders and users are happy with it, you will need to have the template signed off on by a supervisor before it can be made available for use. Once approved, the template's availability needs to be communicated to users and its use strictly enforced.

SUCCESS FACTORS IN USING TEMPLATES

Remember that many document control quality issues start with the incorrect use of templates. Conversely, good template use helps avoid rework and delay.

Successful use of templates depends on a number of factors including the control and distribution of latest templates, training of staff, and enforcement of appropriate template use.

Document templates need to be numbered, their revisions coded and controlled like any other controlled document. Why? Because you don't want anyone to use an outdated revision of templates or make unauthorized changes to them. Every time an originator wants to use a template, they must obtain the latest one from the document control centre or EDMS. It is important to avoid making uncontrolled copies of templates available to document writers to eliminate the risk of using outdated templates. Keep in mind that re-applying the correct template to a document could take hours depending on the sophistication of the template and the size of the document.

Furthermore, it is absolutely important to mandate the use of templates in your document control procedure. Your procedure may include a list of templates available for use and how they can be obtained. You may also find it helpful to provide your users a model completed document for each template to demonstrate what a good document should look like when the template is used appropriately. Model documents can be great tools to communicate to document writers the expected quality and level of detail from a document.

Proactive training and support is the key to achieving consistent use of templates, especially among new staff. Companies often make the mistake of assuming that everyone uses document templates correctly because it is stated in the document control procedure.

The hard reality, however, is that many people have too little time to carefully read and apply such procedures. Or they simply forget the detailed instructions because they don't get to apply them every day. This is where training and active coaching come in.

For training to be effective, the document controller needs to work closely with the Human Resources Department so that new joiners are identified and trained on the company's document control processes and procedures.

Finally, if you are a document controller, you should check for template compliance before distributing a document for review, approval or use. It is useful to have instructions for document controllers describing what needs to be checked (including the correct template use) before issuing a new document and what the accept-reject criteria should be. As key participants in the quality assurance process, document controllers should not be afraid to reject non-compliant templates and documents as long as they are not blocking crucial company activity.

Chapter 7

Document Quality Assurance and Control

DOCUMENT CONTROL CHALLENGES

Ensuring the quality of operation in document control is no easy task. There are many document control challenges that can include any of the three cornerstones: people, process, and technology. A weakness in one often affects the others and leads to more quality issues.

People

Of the three document control cornerstones, the 'people' part is most complex, dynamic, and challenging to get right.

Often the biggest challenge is the fact that many business leaders and decision makers don't seem to appreciate the contribution of good document control to achieving organizational objectives. This lack of understanding often leads to poor attention to document control. This issue, backed by broken processes and poor communication, often creates some of the biggest document control issues. Therefore, document controllers need to be active in influencing key decision makers and other stakeholders to obtain the necessary support.

From a resourcing perspective, a common difficulty is attracting and recruiting skilled document controllers. Finding document controllers with the right experience and competencies can be a daunting task. When you do find and hire them, retention will be a huge challenge due to the highly competitive market. This is true particularly in projects. Many companies, these days, provide skilled document control professionals increasingly attractive career opportunities and pay with the possibility to work internationally.

The main issue with document control is not the big 'people' problems. Instead, it is the innumerable small issues that gradually erode the efficiency of your services, often accounting for the difference between successful and useless document control. The people in your organization have varied roles, interests and expectations, degree of document control awareness, and enthusiasm for the document control function. These differences lead to individually small but cumulatively enormous challenges.

Many 'people' issues arise from users' misunderstanding of their roles and responsibilities, lack of training, and a tendency to fall back into their old habits. These issues lead people to perform their tasks incorrectly or totally ignore them. Documents issued with missing control details (dates, revision number, signatures, etc.), documents written on outdated templates, document changes made without approvals or explanations and incorrect document classification are all examples of poor execution of document control responsibilities.

Process

A comprehensive document control process with clear roles and responsibilities is a prerequisite for a successful document control. A good process coupled with the right technology helps you as a document controller to build credibility and support among senior management and users. On the other hand, a sloppy process, or a good but poorly communicated process, will lead to a number of serious issues.

Common process issues include approach to document review (e.g. parallel versus sequential document commenting), document approval design (e.g. number of required approvals, physical vs electronic signatures), physical document distribution and confidentiality management, the process of keeping document registers and distribution matrices current, document management for concurrent engineering (i.e. where a single document is modified by two or more users or projects at the same time), and decision to (or not to) use the EPC contractor's EDMS (yes, this impacts document control process!). These processes need to be thought through carefully before they are implemented. Document control processes, like any other business process, take significant time and effort to develop and introduce. Changing or modifying them will take quite an effort too.

Technology

'Technology' includes anything that you use to draft, review, approve, distribute and archive documents.

In the past decade, a number of companies have introduced electronic document control systems (EDMS) replacing or downsizing their paper-based practices. EDMS systems can bring a number of benefits to organizations in terms of quicker document reviews and approvals, global document access (if EDMS is web-based), and better access control.

Commonly encountered technology issues are that the acquisition of EDMS that does not fit organizational processes, or is too complex resulting in low user adoption, unauthorized EDMS access and security management, and poor disaster recovery in case of damage to or loss of documents.

QUALITY ASSURANCE AND CONTROL

The best way to eliminate quality issues is to prevent them from happening. This is the essence of quality assurance (QA). Conversely, quality control (QC) determines if any quality issues have already occurred, and takes necessary actions to correct them. You will need both QA and QC to effectively manage your documents, but the most effort should go into QA. Remember the old adage: 'Prevention is better than cure.'

Quality Assurance (QA)

With prevention in mind, quality assurance aims to achieve 'zero defect'. This, ultimately, means no defects in your goods and services as a result of poor document control. It requires that the document control process and tools be followed and used as intended by all participants.

As part of your QA, therefore, it is crucial to be customer focused. It is extremely useful to proactively and regularly obtain feedback from your key stakeholders and users about their document control experiences. Never wait until you have a problem. Instead, stay ahead of your game by regularly engaging your stakeholders not only to prevent problems, but also to take full advantage of improvement ideas and opportunities.

The success of your EDMS depends on the effectiveness of the process behind it. You can't expect your document control to work perfectly while running a broken process. Therefore, it is necessary to continuously improve the process based on changing business needs and user feedback.

Equally important is governance. You need to make sure that your process is supported by consistent and clear policies, procedures, and instructions. A good but poorly communicated process is no better than a bad one. Remember that the creation and use of quality documents is a universal responsibility, and not just the responsibility of document control. Everyone that takes part in the document lifecycle is responsible for assuring the quality of documents. That philosophy needs to be clearly reflected in your governance.

Another key part of quality assurance is the administration of the document control function. You need a well-organized document control practice with clear goals and an action plan to manage all aspects of document control. Your document controllers need to be well trained and motivated to make a difference.

Always keep in mind that the document control requirements of your company will evolve over time. As a result, you need to assess changing needs and continuously improve your services. You must be prepared to provide alternative solutions before problems arise.

Finally, to help you make the most impact, it is crucial to ensure that you have the support of senior management, key players and users in your organization. The support and enthusiasm of key stakeholders often help you to obtain the attention and resources that you need to make a difference in quality assurance.

Quality Control (QC)

Document control issues that are not prevented by your quality assurance efforts will likely result in quality problems. The purpose of quality control is, therefore, to identify and correct these problems. That makes quality control a feedback mechanism telling you which quality assurance areas you can improve to further prevent quality issues.

The next section provides more detail on how to use audits and regular reports to manage document control quality.

Reporting

Reports are important performance monitoring tools. They can be used regularly to track performance, communicate achievements, and drive improvement initiatives.

Commonly used document control reports include an incoming list of documents, a list of all documents (MDR), list of newly generated documents, list of overdue documents, and documents issued to a recipient (e.g. client). You can also decide to report on some of the strategic and operational performance indicators presented later in this chapter. Many document control reports are generated weekly or monthly, while ad hoc reports can be generated as required.

There are several ways that you can draft your document control reports. Important considerations are the requirements of your target audience (e.g. management or client) and the desired frequency of reports.

One reporting option is to design custom-made reports based on input from your target audience. While custom-made reports can be extremely useful, their design and preparation them may require a new computer program or more time.

If you are using EDMS, however, you may not need to design reports from scratch. Instead, you first need to see what readymade reporting capabilities the system already has. Many EDMS systems provide you with standard reports varying from a list of newly issued documents to a list of overdue (late) documents and even reports supported by charts. You can also see if your EDMS has an interface with other reporting tools which may allow you to create customized reports.

Quality Reviews (Audit)

You might want to periodically review the performance of your document control function to see if it meets your standards. The standards set for the document control function may depend on what your company does or what internal and external standards and requirements it needs to satisfy. If you are auditing against a certain standard, you can start by reviewing the requirements stated in the standard and then identify key questions that your review needs to address.

The depth and rigor of your audit depends on a number of factors including the size of your company, the purpose of the audit, and the resources available to you.

You could start with a gap analysis, which is limited to a review of the relevant document control documentation such as document control policies and sample documents. You could also do an internal audit where, in addition to a simple review of documents, you could speak to various participants of the document control process to see if the processes, activities, and responsibilities are clearly understood. Pre-assessment or external audit is another option.

It is important to understand that an audit of the document control function can be part of a company-wide quality audit. As a result, it is always a good idea to check if there is a planned audit in the company before you start planning your own document control department audit.

The list below contains several useful questions that can be asked during an audit. You can modify the audit questions based on the goal of your audit and the unique circumstances of your company.

- Are documents, of both internal and external origin, uniquely identified and is their latest status appropriately reflected (document title and number, revision number, issue date, reason for issue, etc.)?

- Are documents reviewed and approved by the authorized personnel prior to issue?

- Are staff informed when documents are updated and made available?

- Are documents current and within the review date?

- Are documents accessible to the right users at points of use?

- Is there evidence of appropriate document distribution?

- Are documents stored in the proper location and is their security managed?

- Are document control processes, activities and responsibilities clearly defined and understood? Are supporting documents up to date?

- Are obsolete documents, including previous revisions, identified, removed from points of access, and retained as per the defined retention schedule? Are they available for retrieval?

- Is there evidence of a backup procedure for the document control system?

PERFORMANCE INDICATORS

Purpose

Performance indicators are quantitative and qualitative measures used to compare an organization's progress against its goals.

Performance indicators are periodically compared against set goals and targets to see if the organization or function has met its promises. The outcome of this comparison helps to take specific quality assurance or performance enhancement actions to help business functions. Like any other business function, the document control department can benefit from the use of indicators to monitor and improve its performance.

Performance indicators enable evidential based improvement to strategies, structures, processes, or service delivery. For example, you can use your indicator measurements to compare your past and present document control performance and to set more challenging targets for the future. You can even use indicators to compare your performance against those of other organizations or the industry.

Indicators can also be great communication tools on your document control performance and improvement. They can be effectively used to raise the profile of document control as an important partner in the organization by showing your progress and the quality difference you are making. You can also use performance indicators for planning and decision making purposes as well as for document control risk and issues management.

Furthermore, indictors can be used for the performance appraisals and compensation of your document control staff. If your organization one day is on the receiving end of document control services, such as from a design contractor, you can use your performance indicators as part of the expected service-level agreement, which the contractor has to meet in order to be paid.

Types of indicators

Generally, indicators can be either key performance indicators (KPIs) or simple performance indicators.

KPIs are used to measure achievement of your critical success factors (CSFs), which are linked to your organization's objectives and ultimately its vision. Consequently, KPIs usually measure key activities and processes in which your organization must excel in order to achieve its objectives and remain competitive.

KPIs can be used for document control if the document control function makes a direct contribution to the organization's strategic value, and if each KPI can be linked to a critical success factor in addition to just departmental business outcomes.

Whether or not KPIs are used, you might want to consider using operational performance indicators ('operational pointers') which tell you how well your document control function is performing at the day-to-day operation level. Using a combination of strategic and operational performance indicators gives you a good control of both short-term and long-term performance issues.

Performance indicators identification

How do you come up with the performance indicators for your document control activities? This section gives you a starting list of performance indicators. You can also contact other document controllers in your organization or in your professional network to identify additional indicators. But that is the easy part.

For any process, the best performance indicator is the one that measures the outcome(s) the process is designed to create. Therefore, you should really think about what your document control process is meant to achieve given your organization's goals and objectives. You should thoroughly examine your organization's unique situation. What does your organization do or produce? What are its objectives? How does document control contribute to the bottom line? What should be your priorities from a document control perspective?

There is often a tendency to derive performance indicators based on existing document control 'day-to-day' activities. If performance indicators are derived solely from what goes on inside the document control department then broader measures of organizational success will be ignored. That may lead to the use of indicators that fail to support overall business performance.

While you are developing performance indicators, analyse your organization's strategies, plans, objectives and key business processes to see how you can best support them. In addition, research existing or expected statutory, regulatory and industry requirements to identity document control reporting areas. It is also important to identify any existing or potential problem areas which you might want to keep a close eye on through indicators and reporting. You also need to review your function's current inefficient or ineffective practices and see which indicators can be helpful to monitor improvement.

If you are new to the company, it is always good to look at what has been done in the past regarding indicators. A good understanding of departmental reporting history not only gives you an advance start but also lets you know which indicators worked and which did not in the past. This review should give you a good idea about the critical success factors and which areas you need to focus on in addition to a starting list of indicators.

Qualities of good indicators

Keep in mind that performance indicators need to be carefully selected. The use of the wrong performance measures can result in counter-productive work behavior and sub- optimal outcomes. The performance indicators that you select should be:

Few in number: Since indicators measure only key focus areas you only need to monitor a few indicators, whenever possible. The rule of thumb is to limit your performance indicators to between three and five so you know if your document control operation is meeting its most important goals. Managing too many indicators will distract you from day-to-day work or even create confusion among users. In addition, keeping more indicators will cost more money and may introduce unnecessary extra work load.

Clearly defined: To ensure common understanding and consistency in measurement, you need to clearly define the scope of each indicator and how it will be measured. For example, what does 'quality issues' mean in the indicator 'percentage of documents with quality issues'? If you are monitoring 'availability of EDMS to users,' would it count if the EDMS is not available due to scheduled maintenance downtime or an outage on the weekend?

Measurable: Performance indicators must be clear, unambiguous, observable, and as a result, quantitatively or qualitatively measurable with reasonable accuracy. For example, the 'number (or percentage) of documents not in the EDMS' is a poor indicator since measurement will take a long time in large organizations, and the indicator will change before you are done counting.

102   Document Control

Understood: Ensure that all indicators are clearly understood and agreed upon by everyone involved. People that contribute to or are affected by the indicators need to know the purpose of each indicator and how it will be influenced by their behavior. People also need to understand that the purpose of maintaining indicators is not to point blame at them, but to work together to improve organizational performance.

Not counterproductive: Good indicators drive the right behaviors at work and discourage the wrong ones. For example, measuring 'average turnaround time' (i.e. time to sign off on a document) can not only mislead (since often important changes take longer to review and approve) but also create a culture where documents are signed off without proper consideration just to meet due dates.

Cost effective: The measurement of an indicator should not take too long or cost too much. Always remember that measuring performance should assist your daily work and not be significant part of it. As an example, measuring 'time taken from document drafting to approval' may be manageable in a relatively small company. However, monitoring the same indicator in a large organization can be too expensive, if not nearly impossible, given the volume of documents and the complexity of the document control environment.

Communicated: The very idea of monitoring indicators is to drive process or organizational performance by reporting on document control achievements and performance gaps. It is important to make sure that measurements of your indicators, challenges, and suggested improvements are regularly reported to relevant stakeholders and contributors. This will enable you to keep your stakeholders involved and to make your efforts more visible to them.

Governed: Accountability and the responsibility for measuring and reporting on performance indicators needs to be clearly defined and understood. You can document these roles and responsibilities in your document control procedure.

Assessed: The relevance of certain performance indicators may change depending on the maturity of your organization and the document control processes. It is, therefore, essential that you periodically review the applicability of your indicators in light of the changing organizational and business circumstances.

List of performance indicators

A starting list of indicators you can chose from is presented below. It is important to remember that you need to maintain only a limited number of them and ensure that each indicator really adds value to your reporting. Furthermore, note that those terms in the list with an asterisk (*) require careful definition to ensure a consistent and reliable measurement.

- Percentage of documents with quality issues*

- Number of cases of obsolete document usage

- Percentage of documents with too many* reviews before approval (this, for example, indicates coordination and communication issues)

- Percentage of overdue documents (i.e. documents not reviewed or signed off in a timely manner)

- Number of rejected documents per department (tells you which department needs attention or support)

- Percentage of documents handed over in a timely manner to client (delivery)

- Percentage of critical documents approved in a timely manner for start of work (e.g. for construction)

- Percentage of documents made 'as-built'

- Number of documents created within a set time period

- Client/user satisfaction level*

- EDMS uptime* (availability to users)

- Cost* of resources per amount of service* provided (e.g. number of documents issued)

- Document storage costs (paper and electronic)

- Ratio of paper to electronic documents

- Number of identified corrective actions resolved/unresolved

- Time to respond to and correct non-compliance*

- Number of information security or confidentiality breaches

- Percentage of obsolete documents not removed from use

- Percentage of documents not accessed for a set time (e.g. 1 year) (indicates the usefulness or quality of the documents) Investment in document management related education and training (hours per annum, cost and number of staff by course)

Chapter 8

Document Control Procedures

In Chapter 4, we discussed document control procedure as a governance tool and looked at its purpose and commonly expected contents. This chapter talks about writing effective document control procedures.

The document control procedure is an important instrument that tells all participants how documents need to be managed from creation to archival. It helps document controllers set and maintain minimum document control standards.

A typical document control procedure's table of contents will include the topics shown in Figure 8.1. However, there is no hard and fast rule about what to include: you can always add, remove, and customize the chapters and contents to suit your own document control requirements. You can even write separate document control procedures on each one or more of these topics as required, given the size and complexity of your document control environment.

If you believe that any one of the procedure's supporting documents such as the distribution matrix are likely to change often, then it is better to issue them as separate documents from the procedure. If such supporting documents are made a part of the document control procedure, you will have to reissue the entire procedure every time something changes in the supporting document. This frequent document review is likely to introduce costly errors in the procedure and require additional time to review and approve it.

WRITING AN EFFECTIVE DOCUMENT CONTROL PROCEDURE

A good place to start writing a document control procedure is to search for samples on the Internet. A simple search should give you good samples that you can use to shape the content of the procedure you are about to write. You will have to go through the following thinking process in order to fully understand your company's document control requirements and to write a fit-for-purpose procedure. Here are important writing steps.

Define your scope

An explicit scope of the document control process needs to be stated early in your procedure in order to give the reader an unambiguous picture of what the procedure applies to and what it does not.

Ask yourself questions such as:

- Is the procedure going to apply only to your part of the organization (e.g. a project) or the whole company?

- Will the document control procedure apply to technical documents or does it also need to address non-technical documents?

- Are correspondence and other records considered to be 'documents'?

Answering these important questions enables you not only to determine the comprehensiveness of your procedure but also to write a clear and complete guide.

Identify and define all your processes

A good understanding of your processes allows you to write good procedures. While larger organizations often have complex processes for document control, smaller organizations can use simpler processes. In all cases, make sure that you have the complete picture of your processes from document creation to approval, distribution and archival.

At the highest level, think of people, processes and technology. These three elements make document control work. Use the systems approach to identify required inputs and expected outputs of your processes. Your procedure should define what documents (e.g. templates) are consumed as part of the process, and what records (e.g. completed comment forms) are released as outputs. In discussions with your stakeholders, identify required activities in each of the processes. Ask yourself what needs to be done and documented before you can call a document control process complete. Whenever possible, learn more about the process from the process owners themselves and ask them to help write the procedure.

Table of Contents

1. Purpose
2. Scope
3. Reference Documents (i.e. related documents)
4. Definition of Terms and Acronyms
5. Distribution and Intended Audience
6. Roles and Responsibilities
7. Document Preparation and Production
8. Document Numbering, Revision Coding, and Dating
9. Document Review and Approval Process
10. Amending, Updating and Cancelling Documents
11. Internal Document Storage and Access
12. External Documents Management
13. Archival and Disposal of Obsolete Documents
14. Reporting and Performance Indicators
15. Quality Assurance and Control
16. Appendix /Attachments

Figure 8.1: Table of contents for document control procedure

Identify document control roles and responsibilities

An important purpose of document control procedures is to clearly assign roles and responsibilities to various stakeholders. This is the 'people' part of the puzzle. For instance, if a new document is to be created, who will authorize the request? Who writes the document? Who will review and approve it? A RASCI (Responsible, Accountable, Support, Consult and Inform) chart can be a good way to clearly show the roles of individuals and departments for different activities.

No procedure is complete until all relevant roles are identified and clear responsibilities are assigned. Clarity on roles and responsibilities will help you to ensure a smooth and fast document control process without confusion and mistakes.

	Document User	Originator	Reviewer	Approver	Document Controller
Write	C	R		A	IC
Review		A	R	I	I
Approve	I	I	I	R	I
Use	R	I		A	
Distribute	I		I	A	R
Initiate change	C	R		A	
Archive	I		IC		A	R
*R= Responsible *A=Accountable *S=Support *C=Consult *I=Inform						

Table 8.1: RASCI chart of document control roles and responsibilities

Define standards

You need standards for your document numbering, revision numbering, and dating among others. These standards need to be carefully set in order to avoid the pitfalls that we discussed in the previous chapters.

If you are new to the company, don't assume that your previous company's standards 'will just do fine.' Chances are they won't, since every company is unique in some ways. You need to speak to the right people, and get their opinions and feedback on your proposed approaches.

Put together your procedure

Having completed these four steps, you should now have a good idea about what needs to go into the procedure. The writing of the procedure can now begin. When you are done writing, it will have to go through a formal review and approval, just like any other controlled document, before it is distributed for use in the company.

But, what does a good document control procedure look like? Find out the answer in the next section.

QUALITIES OF A GOOD PROCEDURE

A good document control procedure is concise, clear and complete.

Clarity

A procedure is clear if it is written in a simple, understandable language keeping in mind the readers' differences in education, skill level and language proficiency. Your document control procedure will be read and used by a wide range of people in the company ranging from craftsmen in the factory, to design engineers and senior managers, and even staff of your customer or supplier.

Therefore, the procedure should never feel like a scientific article about brain surgery. It should use only simple, common and non-technical words, whenever possible. If you need to use jargon and acronyms, you must explain what they mean somewhere in your procedure, since their meaning may be less clear over time, or vary from one company or department to the other.

A good procedure also uses short sentences, instead of lengthy and complex ones, to clearly guide the reader through a task. To achieve that, start your sentences with a verb and use the active voice to make it clear who is performing the task.

To clarify complex processes, roles and responsibilities, consider using scripted flow charts, swim-lane diagrams and RACI charts. They can be a great way to visually paint a picture of complex ideas.

Conciseness

Conciseness is a no-brainer, and contributes to a procedure's clarity and readability. Winston Churchill once remarked: "The length of this document defends it well against the risk of its being read." You don't want to leave your reader with that sort of feeling. Remember, the type and amount of detail in your procedure will depend on the range of topics covered, the complexity of the document control process, and the organization's staff level of communication skills and culture, among others.

Read the paragraph below.

> The purpose of this procedure is to ensure the documentation and communication of the aforementioned document control tasks, here after referred to as the Required Tasks, in terms that prohibit their execution in an inconsistent manner, wherein such inconsistency may potentially result in the Required Tasks providing an undesirable result or one that is not repeatable or reproducible...

If you have not fallen asleep already, you seriously need to go away and start revising your document control procedure.

In all seriousness, you have to realize that people are often extremely busy and will be turned off by wordy procedures. The main purpose of writing a procedure is that people will read it and apply it to their work. Most people, when faced with lengthy documents, start skimming and skipping important details, which could, in the end, compromise quality and safety. Even worse, people may start creating their own summary or short hand over which you will have no control, and that you may not even know exists.

Therefore, in your procedure leave out activities that are automated by a documentation management tool, and only define tasks that need to be performed by staff.

You should also avoid writing a procedure for everything and expanding on every little detail. The rule of thumb is to solidify into written procedures only those tasks that are important to be consistently performed the same way. A good question to ask yourself before adding any detail to your procedure is: 'Does it really add value to the ultimate quality of work to be performed by the reader?' It is important to remember that while your document control procedure should be concise, it also needs to be sufficiently detailed and explicit to provide clear direction.

In another effort towards conciseness, you can decide whether to combine your document control instructions into one large procedure, or to write separate ones. For example, you may have separate procedures for 'Document Writing', 'Review and Approval', 'Change, and Revision', and 'Document Control and Distribution.

Your decision will most likely depend on how detailed and long each one of these documents is, and whether you want to share only a specific part of the document control procedure with people inside or outside of your company. Keeping separate procedures will help you to limit the review and approval to just a smaller document when something changes in that document. However, whenever possible, it is better to consolidate all document control procedures into one so that people will find all useful information in one document.

ENSURING SUSTAINED COMPLIANCE TO PROCEDURE

Writing a good document control procedure can be a challenge, but is often just the first step. Getting it in every user's mind and making it a habit is a whole new challenge.

As previously stated, your document control stakeholders can be different in many ways. They come from almost every corner of the company. Some are completely new to document control and may need handholding initially. Others are familiar with document control processes, from working in other companies, but may struggle with old habits that creep in from time to time. Another group of stakeholders don't get to work with documents often, so they tend to forget the processes and rules. Others are extremely busy with their own responsibilities and have little time for anything else. All of these people will need your ongoing support and coaching on document control.

Unfortunately, in many organizations document control is not given enough attention until something goes terribly wrong. Usually document control is a support function and not a revenue generating department. Even though the situation is slowly changing, many organizations and projects still focus more on their physical assets rather than the 'information asset' represented by documents. As a result, the document control function may not always have the people, time and other resources it needs to deliver quality service and support.

In any case, given your stakeholders' diversity and the challenges you face, you need to be proactive in using both traditional and creative ways to manage service quality and to reach out to those who need your help.

Traditional ways of implementing document control practices include mandatory training, one-to-one coaching, and brief written guidelines.

A well-designed training program can be an effective first step in enforcing the document control procedure. Training can be delivered in face-to-face sessions or via recorded messages (e.g. videos). Recorded video instructions can be effective in training people with a minimal amount of trainer's time and effort, since the video can be accessed by trainees on demand. If you feel that your document control processes are complex, you can break the training into introductory and advanced levels. It is important that you link the beginner's document control training with the new employee on-boarding process by adding the

'Document Control Awareness' activity on the list of to-do things for new employees. This will ensure that every new employee will receive the required training and briefing on how to create and use documents.

In addition to standard training, you can conduct brief refresher training on specific topics. Video instruction is also excellent for this purpose and people can refer to them at their own convenience.

Brief instructions, such as a one-pager on how to use the EDMS, can also be useful. Like any other service oriented function, the document controller's door needs to be open to allow people to ask questions and to get quick coaching and assistance on document control.

Controlling the quality of documents is another way of ensuring employee's compliance with the company's document control procedures. Document controllers need to take an active role in identifying document quality problems before documents are introduced in the document control system. As mentioned before, a number of things can go wrong with documents including incorrect use of templates, erroneous document identifying details, incomplete review or approval, etc. All errors need to be identified and corrected before documents are distributed to readers.

You can take the document controller's role in quality assurance to the next level by mandating that the document controller to be included as a reviewer in the workflow for all documents. Some companies also require the document controller's signature for every approved document in a bid to ensure document quality. Such practices, while they may add complexity to the workflow, guarantee that the document controller has good visibility of each document from review to approval, and creates the opportunity to identify and point out document quality flaws in a timely manner.

A related traditional quality control method is an audit. Audits can be either formal or informal reviews. Audits can help you to look at all aspects of your document control and to highlight improvement areas.

Always remember to keep a record of quality issues and improvement opportunities you identify as a result of your quality control processes, audits and reviews. You can use these records to later identify the source of the problem and incorporate the solution in your document control procedure or other governance tools. The same records can be further used to improve the purpose and contents of your trainings and coaching activities.

Finally, there are less conventional but more proactive ways to reach and educate your stakeholders on document control.

Placing an eye-catching document control poster by the coffee corner is an example. You can also send out a brief weekly 'Tip of the Week' email on document control highlighting a common issue and a trick or short-cut around it. You can also invite your audience to a brief 'snack and learn' session where you can talk about the latest in document control over free coffee or lunch to your co-workers. You can also take five minutes at a departmental or project meeting to brief your colleagues on key document control issues. These creative ways help you to share information and new developments and to position the document control department as an important and active partner in the organization.

Chapter 9

Project Document Control

Project document control, even though it follows similar document review and approval processes like those discussed in the previous chapters, is distinct in many ways. It is such a specialized and wide-ranging topic that it could easily take a whole new book to discuss.

The intention of this chapter, however, is to introduce the key activities, processes, and challenges in managing documents in a project context.

THE PROJECT ENVIRONMENT

Projects

It is important to realize that projects are temporary endeavors. They are set up to achieve a specific objective. The objective could be to build a new power plant, an oil rig or a refinery, or modify or dismantle an existing facility. When the objective is achieved or abandoned, the project will be closed.

Projects usually go through a pre-defined development lifecycle. They often start with a feasibility study, and then progress through multiple stages including design and development. Construction projects, which will be the focus of this chapter, go through a conceptual study (feasibility study), Front End Engineering & Design (FEED), and execution phases.

A feasibility study is an assessment of the technical, social, environmental and economic viability of a proposed project. It outlines and analyses alternatives to implement the project. It establishes the design requirements of the facilities, narrows the scope of the project, assesses the various engineering alternatives and finally identifies the best scenario.

FEED focuses on specifying the technical scope and requirements of the project, and estimating its approximate investment cost. FEED provides high-level design of the facilities and bridges the gap between feasibility and the detailed design phase. The technical and financial studies done during FEED are used to tender the project work and select one or more construction contractors for the execution of the rest of the project.

The execution phase of a construction project includes the detailed design and actual construction of the facilities. In detailed design, based on the high-level design from the FEED phase, engineers develop comprehensive and in-depth designs and specifications. These design documents (e.g. drawings) and specifications are then used to procure and fabricate pieces of equipment and finally to construct and commission the facility.

Investors continuously monitor the financial, social and political viability of their projects and hold reviews at the end of conceptual design (feasibility study) and FEED stages to decide whether the project should proceed to the next phase or not. Every additional project phase, especially execution, costs more money. Investors, after careful review, may decide to continue with the project, re-conduct the project phase just completed (e.g. FEED), slow it down or scrap it all together.

EPC contractors in projects

Large construction projects usually hire companies known as EPC (Engineer, Procurement and Construction) contractors to design and build facilities. EPC companies are often large firms that execute the project by bringing together a variety of skills in the areas of engineering, project management, procurement and construction.

The EPC contractors are screened, selected and awarded a contract through a structured contractual process. They can be hired to carry out all phases of the project or only part of it, such as the FEED or detailed design and construction part. Depending on the project's size, two or more EPC contractors may be hired to work on the same project phase, especially during the execution phase (i.e. detail design and construction), which is usually the longest and most costly phase of the project.

An EPC contractor, in the process of executing the project, will self-produce and collect a significant number of documents from its vendors and sub-contractors. The volume of documents involved depends on the size and complexity of the project. However, most project documents are generated by equipment vendors and suppliers. Examples of project documents include design drawings, calculations, specifications, installation and maintenance manuals, operating procedures, equipment quality certificates, and even inspection and quality assurance records.

The project team (commonly known as the client or owner's team) is often not directly involved in the day-to-day work of the EPC contractor. Instead, it oversees the contractor's progress to ensure the project is done according to the quality and manner agreed in the contract. It is common in some industries for the client to hire a Project Management Services Contractor (PMSC) that supervises the EPC contractors on the client's behalf. Whether it is the PMSC or the client, one of the key duties is, of course, making sure that the contractor and its vendors create, manage and handover documents to the client as required.

DOCUMENT LIFECYCLE IN PROJECTS

Review and approval

A document prepared by an EPC contractor's discipline will typically first be issued for review by members of the same team. If the document is deemed to affect the work of other disciplines within the contractor's organization (if there is dependency between documents produced by different departments), the document will be issued for review by other relevant disciplines. The review of documents by other disciplines is known as inter-disciplinary commenting or squad check.

At the end of the review period, the originator discipline then consolidates the comments from the various reviewers, resolves any conflicts in the comments, and prepares the revision of the document for the next step. The next step could be another round of review within the same discipline or a squad check. The review process ensures that the document reaches an acceptable level of quality before it progresses to the next stage.

Once the review and update of the document is carried out within the contractor's organization, the document is then issued for review to the clients' organization. Before the end of the review cycle, the 'comments coordinator' from the client side will consolidate their team's comments and send them back to the contractor through document control. The client often uses different 'document return codes' to indicate:

- The client has reviewed the document and has no comment. Work may proceed.

- The client has comments. The contractor may proceed with design at his own risk on the assumption that the client will have no comments or concerns on the document when it is re-submitted.

- The contractor needs to stop the design process and needs to incorporate the client's comments and resubmit for client's review. The document does not meet the client's quality requirements and is therefore rejected.

This cycle of review between the contractor and client teams will continue until the client verifies the quality of the document. Design documents that are verified by the client and approved by the contractor will be released to guide upcoming project activities such as detail design, equipment purchase, fabrication or construction.

There are some documents that the client receives 'for information only' or does not even need to review at all.

In large projects, tens and hundreds of thousands of documents can be produced in a single phase. However, the client will have much fewer staff than the contractor. As a result, they won't have time to review all of the documents that the contractor's and vendors' large teams produce. Given the high volume of documents especially during the detail design and construction phases of the project, the client makes a risk-based decision on the design and engineering documents that they want to review. This decision is an input to creating the DDM so those documents that don't need review are issued to the client just 'for information only.

It is also important to keep in mind that projects have documents that are created, reviewed, approved and used only within the contractor's or client's organization and are not exchanged. Examples include project plans and internal procedures which are strictly for internal use.

While discussing the review and approval of documents, it is important to point out that the client staff are usually not required to approve the EPC contractor's documents for legal reasons. The contractor is ultimately responsible for ensuring the integrity and safety of his designs and the construction work. That means the client staff only review and comment on the contractor's documents in order to help him meet the minimum engineering design requirements. Other than that, the client staff don't sign off the contractor's documents for quality, because doing so may mean a transfer of design liability from the contractor to them.

Many times, in order to expedite the design process, the contractor personnel informally discuss their documents with the client staff. This allows them to improve the quality of the documents without going through the formal review, which in many cases takes at least ten working days. When the client engineer is happy with the quality of the document, the contractor engineer will issue the document for the client review and immediately continue the design work based on the document just issued. The client engineer is expected to have no comment based on the earlier discussion, and at the end of the review period the document can go directly for an approval within the contractor's organization. The important thing is that the contractor engineer needs to informally agree to the expected response date with his counterpart. This will help avoid delays caused by documents unnecessarily falling deeper into the client's organization during the informal review. It is important to note that this practice, while saving project time, may not be totally consistent with the official document control process and could potentially impact quality.

Project document lifecycle and status

In the previous chapters, we said that documents are created, reviewed, approved, used, archived and disposed of. All these phases are enabled through the distribution or movement of the documents. During each phase of their lifecycle, documents take statuses such as 'Issued for Review,' 'Approved,' 'Issued for Information,' 'Cancelled,' or 'Obsolete.

Project documents have the same lifecycle. They are created, reviewed, approved and finally archived and discarded. However, technical project documents such as drawings may have additional statuses as they go through the design and construction process.

Document status naming practices may differ from one industry or company to the other, but the following are the commonly used terms.

Issued for Review: The document is issued for review within the EPC contractor's discipline that prepared the document.

Issued for Inter-disciplinary Review: The document is issued within the EPC contractor's organization for review by other disciplines.

Issued for Client Review (ICR): The document has been reviewed within the contractor's organization and is now issued for the client's comment.

Approved for Design (AFD): The document (usually a drawing or specification), after the required number of commenting and revision by the contractor and client staff, is now complete in all aspects of design and is approved.

Issued/Approved for Construction (AFC): The AFD document is further developed in the detailed design phase, and has been reviewed and approved by the appropriate body (contractor engineer, local governing agencies, etc.) and therefore can be used to build the project facilities.

Documents with status such as 'Approved/Issued for Bidding/Tender" and 'Issued/Approved for Material Purchase' have achieved the required quality level and are ready to serve the purpose indicated in their status title.

As-built (ASB): Sometimes engineers working with Issued for Construction (IFC) documents are forced to make unforeseen design or installation changes in order to accommodate specific challenges at the construction site. These changes need to be identified and reflected in the IFC documents in order for the drawings to fully and accurately represent the technical status of a completed facility as handed over to the client. This process is known as 'as-building' and the documents will have the 'as-built' status at the end of the process.

Such unexpected construction changes are often marked up by the engineer electronically or physically on the printed drawing using different colours. Commonly used colours are red, blue and green. Interestingly, there is no consensus on the meaning of these colours, but the most common practice seems to be that red is for additions, green is for deletions and blue is for additional notes or remarks. Some companies use just red for all. Documents with these design changes will be revised and updated to an 'as-built' status.

Rev	Description
01R	Preliminary Issue for Review
02R	Issued for Inter-disciplinary Review
03R	Issued for Client Review
04A	Approved for Design
05R	Revised and Issued for Review
06A	Approved for Construction
07R	Revised and Issued for Review
Z	As-Built

Figure 9.1: Sample revision codes for technical documents

DOCUMENT TRANSMITTALS AND DOCUMENT DISTRIBUTION

Documents sent from one party to the other, for example from a contractor to a client or from an originator to a reviewer or approver in the same organization, are sent together with a transmittal note. The transmittal note (also known as letter of transmittal or transmittal sheet) is a document delivery note that gives the receiving party the details of the documents enclosed.

Transmittals accompany every document exchange in order to capture the identity of the exchanged documents and keep an auditable trail of the exchange. A single transmittal may accompany two or more documents.

A transmittal issued from one company to the other, as it is between a client and a contractor, is known as an external transmittal. An internal document transmittal is a document exchange within the client's or contractor's organization.

	XYZ Inc							
	TRANSMITTAL NOTE							
Project Name								
Transmittal Number								
Date								
Recipient Names								
1								
2								
3								
4								
No.	Document No.	Rev	Document Title	Transmittal Purpose	No of Pages	No. of Copies	Due Date
1							
2							

Figure 9. 2: Sample electronic transmittal note

Each transmittal note has a unique number and identifies the sender, recipient(s) and the date and time of the exchange. It identifies (title, number, revision, etc.) each document included in the transmittal and lists the purpose of the document issue for each document. The transmittal note further captures the total pages of each document (for initial completeness check by document controller) and shows the provided review period or response due date. Figure 9.2 shows a sample transmittal note.

Many EDMSs enable you to electronically create transmittals, add an EDMS link to the documents you are issuing, and email them directly to the recipients. The recipients can then follow the link or check their inbox in the EDMS to access the documents. In some cases, however, the transmittal sheet needs to be printed out and signed by the recipient and then sent back to the sender as a feedback to confirm that the documents have been received. The date of the receiver's signature, in such cases, marks the start of the document review period. Electronic or signed transmittal notes can be used as a proof of document delivery, notably in case of an audit or legal proceedings.

PROJECT DOCUMENT CONTROL ACTIVITIES

Project document control activities can be discussed either from the client's or the EPC contractor's perspective. In this chapter, we will discuss document control from the client's point of view since it is the client that is responsible for good document control and takes ownership of documents delivered by the contractor at the end of the project.

At the outset, it is important to point out that it is unrealistic to discuss all project document control scenarios in just one chapter. The rest of this chapter we will assume the project under discussion is a large construction project that collaborates with just one EPC contractor in the detail design and construction phase of the project. This project phase is the most complex since it involves the largest number of project partners including equipment and service suppliers and vendors which the contractor will work with. In the project phase, these parties produce most of the project documents as part of the design, purchase and construction processes.

In addition, for the purpose of our discussion, we will leave out the presence of a PMSC or additional EPC contractors in this project phase. However, such a project scenario may involve thousands of people who will contribute to and be affected by the document control process. I hope this scenario is complex enough to give you an idea of how documents are managed in projects. It is important to note that for a number of reasons project document control is more dynamic than, for example, the one in an administrative office setting. While the project document controller's responsibilities essentially remain the same, he or she will have more parties to deal with including contractors, regulators, and their own project teams which might be based in different locations across the globe. It is also true that most project documents are created by the contractor or its suppliers. That often makes the collection of documents from the project partners a significant part of the client's document control activities.

At the highest level, from the client's perspective, there are three key project document control tasks that contribute to effective document control. They are:

- Specifying the client's document control requirements to the EPC contractor

- Supervising the quality of the contractors' document management and delivery, and

- Taking planned and timely handover of project documents from the contractor

Each is discussed in more detail in the following sections.

Specifying project document control requirements

On a typical construction project, the EPC contractor, suppliers and vendors produce a variety of documents and records including design drawings, equipment installation and maintenance manuals, purchase documents, and quality assurance records required to design, build and manage the facilities. At the end of the project, most of these documents will be handed over to the client. The client will need such documents to demonstrate to local authorities and others stakeholders that the facility is built according to the design and specifications, and that it can be operated and maintained safely.

Specifying project document control requirements

On a typical construction project, the EPC contractor, suppliers and vendors produce a variety of documents and records including design drawings, equipment installation and maintenance manuals, purchase documents, and quality assurance records required to design, build and manage the facilities. At the end of the project, most of these documents will be handed over to the client. The client will need such documents to demonstrate to local authorities and others stakeholders that the facility is built according to the design and specifications, and that it can be operated and maintained safely.

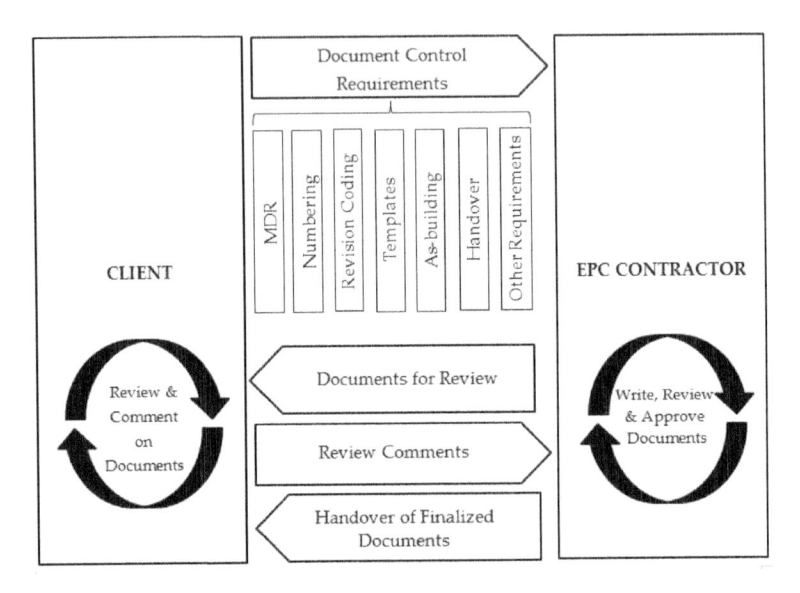

Figure 9.3: Document control interaction between client and contractor

As a preparation for the detail design and construction phase of the project, a very detailed and usually tens and hundreds of millions of dollar-worth contract will be signed with the selected (i.e. bid winner) EPC contractor that will design and build the facilities. The contract covers the scope, terms and conditions of the project work including the creation and management of documents.

Inclusion of clear document management requirements and instructions in the contract at this early stage is essential and is your best opportunity to formally communicate to the contractor your document-related needs. Failure to do so often leads to quality issues, schedule delays and unexpected payment requests by the contractor for additional document control services. This may result in the breakdown of the working relationship between the client and the contractor teams. Therefore, it is very important to make sure that the contract clearly mentions all of the document control requirements expected of the contractor.

The EPC contractor, in turn, is responsible for ensuring that its suppliers manage their documents according to the client's specifications. Usually the client can't instruct the project suppliers directly on document control issues, since the suppliers' contractual relationship is with the EPC contractor and not with the client. Therefore, all document control directions need to be given to the suppliers and vendors by the contractor.

Among document control requirements commonly included in the contract are the numbering of documents, coding of revisions, the distribution of documents for client's review, the contractor-to-client document transmittal process description, the resolution of comments, reporting and progress monitoring, and the final document handover process and timing. Other requirements covered by the contract are the use of document templates (often provided by the client), list of document types and classification, hardcopy requirements (i.e. requiring all documents in hardcopy will raise costs for the client), as-building requirements by document type (list of document types that will need to be delivered in as-built state).

Early in the project, the EPC contractor's document control center prepares the necessary document control procedures and instructions based on the client's document control requirements. Examples of these procedures are the project document numbering procedure, project document management procedure, project document preparation, document issue and review procedure, and the project handover dossiers preparation procedure. These documents have to be reviewed and agreed upon by the client before they can be distributed for use.

Specifying document control requirements can be deceptively straight forward. Here is a simple example that could go horribly wrong.

Many finalized project documents are delivered in native format. Assume that you specify to your contractor that certain documents be delivered in Portable Document Format (PDF). What kind of PDF do you want it to be? Does it need to be text-searchable PDF so that you will be able to electronically search the documents? Should the PDF be produced from the original native document or a scanned document? What should be the minimum resolution if it is a scanned document? Should it include 'bookmark' if it exceeds a certain number of pages? Which application and version should the PDF be compatible with?

It is important to clearly and exhaustively specify document requirements for all physical and electronic files including digital photos and videos when appropriate. It might also be useful to specify 'interim' and 'final' requirements since what users need during the project could be different from what is required at its completion. For example, native database files of two-dimensional (2D) drawings are often required only at the end of the project. During the project, AUTOCAD and PDF of the drawings could suffice for client's review.

When specifying your (i.e. the client's) document control requirements, you need to consider your organization's information management strategy (e.g. minimize paperwork, assurance of quality through periodic contractor document quality checks, etc.), document management standards and practices, as well as any state and industry regulatory requirements. This allows you to develop a complete set of requirements that will meet your project's document requirements.

Once the project's document control requirements are documented and communicated to the contractor, it will be important to discuss in detail with the contractor's document control focal point if there are any requirements that can't be satisfied by the contractor's document control processes and technology. Such gaps in requirements need to be identified at the start of the project and solutions and workarounds need to be agreed upon and put in place as soon as possible. Once the client's and contractor's document control expectations are aligned, the document control activities can begin.

One important choice that needs to be made before a new project phase begins with a new contractor is deciding if the client and contractor should share the same EDMS.

Document review and approval can be made more efficient if both parties use the contractor's system. Conversely, if the client and contractor use their own EDMSs, additional hours and even days may be required for the contractor's document controller to send the documents to the client, and for the client document controller to upload the documents into the client's EDMS and distribute the documents. It will take as long to repeat the process. This type of arrangement will require more document controllers to support the project during peak times or risk running into significant delays.

The risks of sharing the contractor's EDMS need to be appropriately assessed before making a decision. The main concerns are the potential consequences of a legal dispute in the middle of the project. Although there is usually only a slight risk, if a legal battle ensues, you as the client could be cut off from the EPC contractor's EDMS with no access to your documents and their previous revisions. The impact of this risk can be reduced by ensuring that the contractor hands over documents on a regular basis as the project progresses. While using the contractor's EDMS, the client may not have full visibility of the documents and their progress. This is because the reporting abilities will remain in the hands of the contractor, and the client may not always have the means to verify the reported status of documents (e.g. the number of documents completed by a certain date).

If the decision is to use the contractor's EDMS, then you need to make sure that the system is well supported in terms of information security, access control and tracking, back-up, disaster recovery and software upgrade. A simple audit of the contractor's document control processes and technology at the start of the project can give you a peace of mind.

As mentioned earlier, an alternative to using the contractor's EDMS is to bring contractor-produced documents into the client's EDMS for the project team's review. This is usually the only option if the project has two or more EPC contractors. EPC contractors, unless they are teaming up as one joint venture to execute the project, do not want to store their documents in the same EDMS with other contractors since they often work with proprietary information and are competitors with one another. You also want to avoid contractors blaming the EDMS provider contractor in case of EDMS failure or document control issues. Conversely, if you are working with just one main contractor as we assumed earlier, using your own EDMS will give you good control and visibility of the contractor's documents and their progress.

Like any other quality assurance exercise, you need to invest sufficient time and effort in specifying your document control requirements upfront before the contract is signed with the EPC contractor. That will allow you to spend significantly less effort in controlling quality later in the project. Remember that most of your effort should be in quality planning and assurance (i.e. specifying requirements, providing proactive feedback and guidance to contractor), and not in quality control (i.e. resolve quality issues after they occur).

Supervising contractors' document management and delivery

Effective document control requires an end-to-end understanding of document flow within projects. Good project document control relies on solid process and governance tools, and active engagement and follow up of EPC contractors' document management performance. Here are three essential steps you need to take so as to ensure that there is functional document control in a project.

Build the Master Document Register (MDR):

The identification of expected documents is one of the first activities usually done early in a new project phase. The expected document deliverables are identified based on the high level deliverables listed in the agreed contract between the client and the contractor. The completion of a single project deliverable may require the creation or delivery of two or more document deliverables depending on the design and engineering processes and standards employed on the project.

Once the deliverables are identified and agreed upon, they will be listed in the MDR for tracking and control purposes. The format and content of the MDR, which often contains the document number, title, revision number, status, expected (forecast) and actual delivery dates for each document, has to be reviewed and verified by the client. The document delivery date in the MDR helps document owners to plan, monitor and expedite document creation and review (turnaround time). In addition, delivery dates enable the MDR to be used as a progress measurement tool especially during the design phase of the project where documents are the only deliverables expected from the contractor.

Once the client and contractor agree on the format of the MDR and its list of documents, the MDR is frozen and any change is managed through a formal management of change process that requires both the client's and contractor's approval. This control ensures the integrity of the MDR. Approved additions to or removal of documents from the MDR can be made on a weekly or monthly basis as agreed between the client and the EPC contractor. The contractor owns the MDR and applies agreed changes to the MDR. Refer to Chapter 4 for more information on the MDR.

Create Document Distribution Matrix (DDM):

At the start of a project, the contractor and client need to work together and create an agreed document distribution matrix (DDM), which was discussed in depth in Chapter 4. The DDM allows the distribution of the right documents to the right individuals on the project both within and across the contractor and client organizations.

XYZ Inc — ABC PROJECT Master Document Register

Document No.	Rev	Document Title	Status	Forecast Date	Actual Date	EDMS Link
ABC-FIN-0001-001	2A	Project Finance Control Procedure	Approved	31-Mar-2015	27-Mar-2015	Link
ABC-PRS-0004-009	4A	Risk Management Procedure	Approved	12-Feb-2015	20-Feb-2015	Link
ABC-PEG-0011-013	2R	Process Engineering Delivery Plan	Issued for Review	22-May-2015		Link
ABC-CEG-0002-002	6A	Construction Specifications	Approved for Construction	17-Apr-2015	17-Apr-2015	Link
ABC-PEG-0003-004	3R	Onsite Pipeline Route	Issue for Client Review	29-May-2015		Link

Figure 9.4: Sample project MDR

Create (key) performance indicators and reports:

The client and contractor document controllers, together with the project management, are tasked with creating the necessary performance indicators and progress reports.

Indicators and reports that allow you to effectively control your documents are discussed in more detail in Chapter Seven. You can always start with leveraging the information contained in the project MDR. The MDR can be a powerful source of information which you can use to measure and report on project progress based on the completion status of project documents. The MDR can be used to generate a number of reports including the number of the weekly or monthly newly created documents, or the number of those issued or approved within a certain period. You can also use the MDR to report on overdue documents- documents that are not started, reviewed or approved in a timely manner.

When it comes to the choice of performance indicators and reports, the key is to monitor those few critical areas that matter most. Indicators and reports need to be understood by all stakeholders so that they can contribute positively towards them.

Periodical document handover

Projects increasingly demand EPC contractors to hand over completed documents periodically, fortnightly or monthly. It is important to note the difference between document transmittal and document handover. Document transmittal refers to any transfer of project documents, including those under review, from the client to the contractor, or vice-versa. Document handover, on the other hand, is the delivery of finalized documents (e.g., approved, approved for construction or as-built) documents to the client by the contractor. Final document handover is a form of transmittal but applies only to completed documents.

Periodic or even better continuous handover of documents by the contractor allows the client to uncover quality problems early and to avoid last minute negative quality surprises at project close.

Handover of completed documents can be organized by discipline or project milestone, and could be made in batches where a group of related documents is very large. In some industries, in addition to regular periodic handover, document handover from contractor to client may be based on project completion milestones. For example, in oil and gas facilities construction projects, key milestones are Mechanical Completion, Ready for Commissioning and Ready for Start-Up. Documents that support successful completion of these milestones will need to be finalized and handed over to the client.

Once documents are handed over, the client's document control team, together with colleagues from various departments, will conduct quality checks on the documents. At this point, documents are reviewed and approved and technically complete, so the quality control focuses on elements such as the use of templates and the correct classification of documents.

At the end of the project, the client has to make sure that all documents are complete and delivered as per the MDR. If the contractor's EDMS was used, the contractor needs to provide the document metadata so that the documents will be bulk-uploaded into the client's EDMS using a bulk-upload tool.

It is important to keep in mind that, depending on the project, an additional project-to-owner handover may be required. For instance, let's say a project that adds new facilities to an existing nuclear plant is completed. This means that the project (i.e. client) will need to hand over all required documents to the operator of the nuclear plant since these documents will be needed to run and maintain the facility. Note that the clients' and operator's document control processes, standards and environments (e.g. EDMS) can be different- a point to remember while initially specifying your document control requirements.

Many of these documents such as drawings, datasheets, and installation manuals that are required for operations and maintenance will be pushed into the plant's live EDMS and physical library where they will be accessible to the plant's operators and maintenance staff. Others such as project administration (e.g. plans, schedules, reports), quality assurance and control 'documents' (e.g. welding and test records) and all older revisions of documents will be archived in case they are needed in the future.

Remember that valuable project documents might be re-used on future projects. Therefore, the Project Manager should ensure there are no ownership or confidentiality issues and that replicable documents are transferred to, ideally, a knowledge management repository.

CHALLENGES IN PROJECT DOCUMENT CONTROL

Since multiple parties, including the client, contractor and vendors, are involved in a single project at the same time, project document control can be complex and challenging. On a typical large project, the document controller faces many more challenges which require careful thinking and an effective approach.

Poor communication of requirements

As indicated earlier, many, if not most, project document control challenges arise from incomplete or incorrect document control requirements passed to the EPC contractor.

In many projects, the client's document control requirements are not fully gathered, documented and agreed with the contractor. In some cases, they are completely ignored and not communicated to project partners until problems surface late in the project. This is often because the scope and complexities of creating, controlling and delivering documents are underestimated.

Take a very simple example. Everyone on a design and construction project knows that electronic documents have to be handed over to the client at the end of the project. But is it clear if hard copy documents will be needed at all? Chances are that operations-critical documents such as emergency procedures will need to be made available in hardcopy for use in the case of power failure. How many hard copies of which documents are needed? Do any of your documents require translation to another language? There are many questions. A good requirement document for document control (i.e. contractual scope of work) covers all of the client's needs and is never an overkill.

Clients that work more closely with their contractors also ensure document control requirements are cascaded down to sub-contractors, vendors and suppliers so that documents from these parties are delivered correctly and on time. These requirements are known as Vendor Document Requirements (VDR). VDRs are issued to vendors that supply equipment and materials to your project. For instance, together with a piece of equipment, you expect the vendor to provide you with installation, operation and maintenance manuals and drawings, and possibly many other documents. Such requirements need to be identified and passed to the vendor through your contractor before purchase of the equipment is agreed upon.

Poor follow up and Quality Assurance

The other common document control challenge in projects is the lack of follow up on what the contractor does in terms of document delivery.

In the past, many projects waited until the end of the project for the contractor to deliver documents. However, clients learned the hard way that this gave them little time to identify and remedy quality issues.

Clients increasingly require contractors to deliver completed documents periodically and progressively. This allows the client's document controllers to see if the documents use agreed templates, numbering and revision coding standards, document classifications, metadata etc. As a client, early access as to as many documents as possible will give you more time for quality assurance and additional leverage if a legal battle breaks out in the middle of the project. Whenever possible, documents and their expected completion date need to be planned and their delivery should be scheduled and followed up on.

The client also needs to set and agree up front with the contractor on the document quality accept-reject criteria and put them to work. Contractor's and vendor's documents need to be checked for quality and issues need to be collaboratively addressed to find a lasting solution.

Poor document control process

Some of the costliest project document related problems come from unintended use of obsolete documents, especially during the purchase, fabrication and construction phases where most of the capital expenditures are made.

While executing projects, dozens of people may depend on a single design document to do their job, and many of them may need to keep a paper version while working at the project site. This creates a unique challenge where distributing a new document revision and collecting older ones becomes a time critical and enormous task.

Ways to communicate such changes include team meetings, which are usually the most practical and quickest, or even phone calls and emails. But the unfortunate fact is that every now and then obsolete documents are unintentionally used by uninformed staff causing projects delays and additional costs.

Limited focus on the 'Information Asset'

Another common challenge in project document control is project leaders' reluctance to invest time and resources on document control. Often, both the client and EPC contractor are focused on delivering the 'physical asset' but not on the 'information asset' of which documents are an important part.

For example, it is common to see projects avoid an initial, small up-front investment on EDMS only to find themselves scrambling to locate missing documents, or trying to migrate their now thousands of documents to a proper EDMS in the middle of the project. Many times, the document control department, like many other support functions, is considered a 'cost centre' and not really a division that actually helps save money. The result is a resource-constrained document control department.

Sometimes, clients attempt to influence contractors to pay more attention to documents by imposing a penalty for incomplete document delivery. But the harsh reality is that such penalties are often too small and contractors decide to take the penalties instead of going through the difficulty of meeting their document delivery commitments. A smarter approach will be to link all contractor payments to document delivery milestones. If documents are not delivered as part of the completed piece of work, the contractor won't be paid, even when a technical landmark is achieved.

ABOUT THE AUTHOR

Dawit Kassa is an Information Management professional for the design and construction of facilities. He is also a PMI-certified IT Project Manager and currently leads a project to design and build advanced construction and asset document and data management systems. His past professional experiences include multiple roles as Information Management Business Analyst, IT Business Analyst and Project Manager working on large oil and gas facilities and projects.

Contact the Author

Thank you for reading this book. If you enjoyed it, please take a moment to leave a review online at Amazon.

If you have comments on how to improve this book, kindly inform the author at thedocumentcontrolbook@gmail.com. Your contribution is much appreciated as it will help improve the Document Control profession.

Thank you.

Index

Approval 39, 40

Approver 19, 39, 40

Archival 44-6

Centralization 24

Challenges in document control 91-3, 134-7

Change request form 33-4

Change tracking 24, 36, 38, 42-3

Classification of documents 9-10

Cover page 84-5

DDM (Document Distribution Matrix) 43-4, 57-8

Documents 4, 8, 10

Document control 13
> Benefits 14-7;
> Organization of 58, 59;
> Principles 23; Process 21-2, 24, 52; Purpose 13;
> Standards 25-7

Document Controller 20, 59-60

Document Coordinator 20

Document Creation Form 30

Document Distribution Matrix *see 'DDM'*

Document Number Request Form 70

Document Review Form 37

Documentation 1, 2, 4

Document title (name) 23, 31

Document vs record 4, 6, 8-9

Distribution of documents 41-2

Disposal 44-6

EDMS 23, 27, 40-42, 56

Electronic Document Management System *see 'EDMS'*

Identification of documents 23

Governance 49, 50

Information Security 11, 17, 43

Lifecycle 21, 29, 120-2

Master Document Register (MDR) 29

Metadata 74-6

Number, of document 23-4

Numbering documents
> Centralization 69;
> Intelligent vs non-intelligent 70; Product-based 73, 74; Project documents 67-9, 73-4

Obsolescence 44-6

Originator 18

Owner of document 19

Performance indicators 98
> Example 103-4
> Good indicators 101-3;
> Identification 100

Index

    Purpose 98; Types 98

Plan 50

Principles of document control 23

Procedure for document control 24, 52-5, 105;
    Contents 107; Ensuring compliance 111-4; Qualities of good procedure 109-111; Writing of 106

Process in document control 21, 22, 24, 52

Project document control 115

Quality assurance 94, 95

Quality control 95, 96

Quality Management System Triangle 71

Quality review (Audit) 96

Records 5, 8

Reporting 95

Review of documents 32-8

Reviewer 18

Revision date 23

Revision number 23

Revision numbering 76

Revision record 39

Revision record sheet 25

Roles in document control 17-21, 59-60

Signatures 40

Standards, documents control 25-7

Strategy 49-51

Technology 22-3

Template
    Benefits of 30, 82-3; Example of 85; How to create 87; Parts of 81, 83; Success factors 89-90

Title see Document title

Transmittals 122-4

Types of documents *see* 'Classification of documents'

Uncontrolled documents 7

Usage 41-42

User 19

Printed in Great Britain
by Amazon